A DIVINE SOCIETY

The Trinity, Community and Society

Dave Andrews

WIPF & STOCK · Eugene, Oregon

Wipf and Stock Publishers
199 W 8th Ave, Suite 3
Eugene, OR 97401

A Divine Society
The Trinity, Community and Society
By Andrews, Dave
Copyright©2008 by Andrews, Dave
ISBN 13: 978-1-61097-856-9
Publication date 12/1/2011
Previously published by Frank Communications, 2008

PREVIEWS

The doctrine of the Trinity — that God is one yet three and three without ceasing to be one — is for many people the most perplexing of all beliefs. How does one make sense of it?

Most believers accept the doctrine, but not many are able to say why they do so or what, if any, practical significance it has for daily living. Not so Dave Andrews. He has meditated long and hard on what this most mysterious and beautiful of religious beliefs means, not just at a theoretical or speculative level — but also at a practical, down-to-earth level.

The triune God, he explains, is a profoundly relational or communitarian Being. Consequently those made in this God's image are also inherently relational beings. We can therefore learn much about what is means to live together healthily in community by reflecting on what we know of God's triunity, as well as what we know of human sociability. Andrews explores these matters in an engaging blend of storytelling, personal experience, theological reflection and pungent social analysis. Over and over again he shows how the Trinity, far from being some mathematical abstraction, is actually *an indispensable paradigm for living together in love in a cruel, violent and lonely world*.

Dr Chris Marshall
St John's Senior Lecturer in Christian Theology
Religious Studies Department
Victoria University of Wellington
Wellington, New Zealand

Dave Andrews is one of Australia's most innovative community workers. His vision for social change, however, comes out of a well articulated theological vision. Dave clearly demonstrates that Jesus' vision of the in-breaking reign of God rooted in Trinitarian theology can be the inspirational centre for contemporary community work. This challenging piece of integrated writing can be *a guide to all who seek to bring the shalom of God to all the places of pain and injustice in our world.*

Dr Charles Ringma
Professor Emeritus
Regent College, Vancouver, Canada

When I met Dave Andrews a few years ago, I could feel the fire burning in him. Then I heard him speak. Then I read his books. Ever since, he has been and continues to be a major inspiration for my life and work. It's natural to think of Dave as a prophet: his fiery passion, his concern for justice, the way his life speaks even more eloquently than his words. But Dave is also a teacher, drawing from some of the most seminal theologians of today along with classic theologians from Christian history, and making them accessible to a wide audience. Divine Society *offers a powerful example of what a prophet and a teacher can mean to the church today.*

Brian McLaren
Pastor (crcc.org)
Author (anewkindofchristian.com)

ACKNOWLEDGEMENTS

I would like to acknowledge my appreciation for Tony Kelly, recently retired Senior Lecturer in Community Work at the University of Queensland. It was Tony who first encouraged me to think seriously about community in trinitarian terms.

I would also like to thank Brian McLaren, Chris Marshall and Charles Ringma for reading an early manuscript and giving me some of their initial responses. I have rewritten sections of the text with their comments in mind, and the book is better for it. However, I accept full responsibility for any inadequacies that still remain.

And I would also like to thank Pieter and Elria Kwant for the work they did on the book's publication; Isobel Stevenson for doing the original editing; Kris Argall for doing the final editing; Hugh Todd for doing the cover design and typography, and Frank Communications for arranging publication.

CONTENTS

INTRODUCTION TO DAVE ANDREWS FOR THE 2012 DAVE ANDREWS LEGACY SERIES

INTRODUCTION: 'EVERYBODY LOVES COMMUNITY' 1

PART ONE: THE TRINITY AS AN ICON OF COMMUNITY 7

A. AN ICON OF COMMUNITY 8
    Rublev's Icon 10
B. THE TRINITY AS PERSONS 16
C. THE TRINITY AS PERSONS IN RELATION 17
D. THE TRINITY AS THREE IN ONE 18
E. GENDER EQUITY IN THE TRINITY 19
F. GENUINE EQUALITY IN THE TRINITY 20
G. GRACIOUS INCLUSIVITY IN THE TRINITY 22

PART TWO: A DIVINE MODEL FOR HUMAN COMMUNITY 25

1. THE CREATOR 28
    A. The Theological Perspective 29
    B. The Eco-Economic Perspective 33
    C. The Socio-Political Perspective 42
2. THE LIBERATOR 46
    A. The Critique of the System 55
    B. The Charisma of Compassion 63
    C. The Catalyst For Transformation 70
3. THE SUSTAINER 79
    A. The Source Of Vitality and Sensitivity 80
    B. The Essence Of Unity And Diversity 90
    C. The Soul Of Originality And Ingenuity 95

PART THREE: AN IMAGINATIVE METHOD FOR COMMUNITY DEVELOPMENT *101*
A. HEARING OUR CALL TO BE 'ECCLESIA' *102*
B. SEEING OUR SELVES AS 'YEAST IN THE DOUGH' *110*
C. ACTING AS 'LITTLE BROTHERS AND SISTERS OF JESUS' *117*
D. TURNING OUR WORLD 'UPSIDE DOWN AND INSIDE OUT' *123*
    i. A Passion for Transformation *124*
    ii. Attention to Preparation *126*
    iii. Sensible Long-Term Strategy *128*
    iv. Practical Short-Term Tactics *131*
    v. Blood, Sweat and Tears *140*

CAUTION: 'THOSE WHO LOVE COMMUNITY DESTROY COMMUNITY; ONLY THOSE WHO LOVE PEOPLE CREATE COMMUNITY' *153*
    On creating a safe space *153*
    On extending acceptance *154*
    On expressing respect *155*
    On exercising care *156*
    On enabling participation *158*
    On embodying justice *159*
    Towards a global ethic *161*

REFERENCES *165*

Introduction to Dave Andrews for the 2012 Dave Andrews Legacy Series

I KEPT SEEING THIS guy on the shuttle bus - long hair, graying beard, a gentle 60's-70's feel to him. He seemed thoughtful, intense, friendly, and quiet, like he had a lot on his mind, as did I. Even though I saw him nearly every time I boarded the shuttle bus, we didn't speak beyond him smiling and saying, "G'day" and me nodding and saying, "Hey" as we boarded or disembarked.

It was my first time at Greenbelt, a huge festival about faith, art, and justice held every August in the UK. I had always heard great things about the event and so was thrilled when I was invited to speak. I was just as thrilled to get a chance to hear in person some musicians and speakers I had only heard about from a distance, so I went through the program and marked people I wanted to be sure not to miss.

It was near the end of the conference when a friend told me to be sure to catch an Australian fellow named Dave Andrews. "I've never heard of him," I said. "Oh, he's a force of nature," my friend said. "Kind of like Jim Wallis, Tony Campolo, and Mother Teresa rolled up into one." How could I not put a combination like that in one of the last free slots on my schedule?

I arrived at the venue a few minutes late and there he was, the bearded guy from the bus. Thoughtful, intense, and friendly, yes — but *quiet* he was not. He was nearly exploding with passion — passion and compassion, in a voice that ranged from fortissimo to fortississimo to furioso. How could a guy churning with so much hope, love, anger, energy, faith, fury, and curiosity have been so quiet and unassuming on the bus?

He was a force of nature indeed, evoking from his audience laughter, shouts, amens, reverent silence, and even tears before he was done. He spoke of justice, of poverty, of oppression, of solidarity across religious differences, of service, of hope, of celebration, of the way of Jesus.

As I listened, I wanted to kick myself. *This is the most inspiring talk I've heard at this whole festival. Why did I miss all those opportunities to get to know this fellow on the bus? Now the festival is almost over and I've missed my chance!*

Later than evening, I boarded the shuttle bus for the last ride back to my hotel, and there sat Dave and his wife, Ange. I didn't miss my chance this time. I introduced myself and they reciprocated warmly.

I was a largely unknown American author at the time and hardly known at Greenbelt, much less in Australia, so I'm quite certain Dave and Ange had never heard of me. But they couldn't have been kinder, and as we disembarked, he pulled two books from his backpack and told me they were a gift.

The next day when I flew home from Heathrow, I devoured them both on the plane. First, I opened *Not Religion, But Love* and read it through from cover to cover. Then I opened *Christi-anarchy* and couldn't put it down either. When my plane landed, I felt I had been on a spiritual retreat . . . or maybe better said, in a kind of spiritual boot camp!

Things I was thinking but had been afraid to say out loud Dave was saying boldly and confidently. Ideas I was very tentatively considering he had already been living with for years. Complaints and concerns I only shared in highly guarded situations he was publishing from the housetops. Hopes and ideals I didn't dare to express he celebrated without embarrassment.

I think I gave him a copy of one or two of my books as well, and I guess he was favorably impressed enough that we stayed in touch and a friendship developed. I discovered that we were both songwriters as well as writers, that we both had a deep interest in interfaith friendships, that we both had some critics and we both had known the pain of labeling and rejection.

Since then, whatever he has written, I've been sure to read . . . knowing that he speaks to my soul in a way that nobody else does.

We've managed to get together several times since our initial meeting in England, in spite of the fact that we live on opposite sides of the planet. We've spoken together at a few conferences on both hemispheres, and I had the privilege of visiting him in Brisbane. I've seen the beautiful things he has been doing in a particularly interesting and challenging neighborhood there, walking the streets with him, meeting his friends, sensing his love for that place and those people. He's been in my home in the US as well, and we've been conspiring for some other chances to be and work together in the future.

In my speaking across North America, I frequently refer to Dave's work, but until now, his books have been hard to come by. That's why I'm thrilled to introduce this volume to everyone I can in North America.

Yes, you'll find he's one part Tony Campolo, one part Jim Wallis, and one part Mother Teresa, a force of nature, as I was told.

You'll also find he is a serious student of the Bible and a serious theological sage — the kind of reflective activist or thinker-practitioner that we need more of.

In a book like *Christi-anarchy*, he can boldly and provocatively unsettle you and challenge you. Then in a book like *Plan Be*, he can gently and pastorally encourage and inspire you. Like the central inspiration of his life, he is the kind of person to confidently turn over tables in the Temple one minute and then humbly defend a shamed and abused woman from her accusers the next.

You'll see in Dave's writings that he is highly knowledgeable about poverty, ecology, psychology, sociology, politics, and economics . . . not only from an academic standpoint, but also from a grass-roots, experiential level. His writing on these subjects grows from what he has done on the ground . . . for example, nurturing a community network that is training young adults to live and serve among the supervising homes for adults who are learning to live with physical and psychiatric disabilities, encouraging small businesses to hire people who others would consider unemployable and developing a non-profit solar energy co-op for local people.

Dave's writings and friendship have meant so much to me. I consider him a friend and mentor. Now I am so happy that people across North America can discover him too.

You'll feel as I did - so grateful that you didn't miss the chance to learn from this one-of-a-kind, un-categorizable, un-containable, wild wonder from Down Under named Dave Andrews.

Brian D. McLaren
author/speaker/activist (brianmclaren.net)

INTRODUCTION

'EVERYBODY LOVES COMMUNITY'

Everybody loves community.

According to sociologists Colin Bell and Howard Newby, 'everyone — even sociologists (who usually like to sit on the fence) — want to live in community.'[1]

In his book *Keywords: A Vocabulary of Culture and Society*, Williams reports that the word 'community' — 'unlike all other terms of social organisation (such as 'group', 'party', 'network', 'association', or 'institution' etc.) — is never...used unfavourably.'[2]

I think it is probably an exaggeration to say the word 'community' is 'never used unfavourably', but it is true to say that it is seldom used unfavourably. And the reason for that is because the word 'community' is essentially a heartfelt word — like 'love', 'romance', 'friendship', 'marriage' or 'family' — which has deep, positive, passionate connotations for most of us most of the time.

I can think of many examples where people have talked unfavourably about issues to do with their community, or about the leadership, direction, and/or organisation of their community; however, I can think of only one example of people talking unfavourably about the notion of community itself. And that was about the 'communities in Queensland' — the state of Australia where I live — where the word 'community' was a euphemism for a reservation run by the state for aborigines, who had been removed forcibly from their land at the point of a gun. So the only example I've come across myself — where people do not talk favourably about 'community' — is where the word 'community' was political double-speak for the destruction of a much-loved community.

When we talk about a community, we are usually talking about a particular context in which we feel at home — 'a place, or a group of people, or a tapestry of meaningful relationships which creates a gracious space that embraces us in a strong-but-gentle, undeniably-beautiful sense of belonging'.

David Clark says it well in *Basic Communities*:

community [is] essentially a sentiment which people have
about themselves in relation to themselves: a sentiment
expressed in action, but still basically a sentiment or a
feeling...People have many feelings, but there are two
essential feelings for the existence of community: a sense of
significance and a sense of solidarity.[3]

§

Aussie commentator, Hugh Mackay, says that human beings are like mobs of kangaroos, because — like them — 'we are creatures who thrive on our connections with each other. We are at our best when we are fully integrated with the herd; we are at our worst when we are isolated.'[4] In his book *Bowling Alone*, Robert Putnam observes that

1. *We are most healthy when we are most connected.* Due to the encouragement of healthy norms, assistance in ill health, advocacy for proper healthcare, and 'herd immunity', people who are connected are less likely to suffer heart attacks, strokes, cancer — even colds! They are also two to five times less likely to die prematurely.[5]
2. *We are most happy when we are most connected.* The best single global indicator of happiness is connectedness. Those who have strong relationships with family and friends are much less likely to experience loneliness, low self-esteem, eating and sleeping disorders, and sadness and depression, than those with weak relationships.[6]
3. *We are most honest when we are most connected.* In relationships, long-term credibility is worth a lot more than any gain from short-term treachery. This explains why there are a lot fewer unreliable used cars returned to second-hand dealers in small-town communities.[7]
4. *We are most generous when we are most connected.* The most common reason for giving is being asked. The most common reason for not giving is not being asked. People are more likely to be asked if they are in contact with others. Thus, people in clubs

and churches are ten times more likely to give help than those who are not.[8]

5. *We are most prosperous when we are most connected.* When people know one another, they are much more likely to share access to jobs, promotions, bonuses, and other benefits.[9] Moreover, when people trust one another, there is a significant reduction in expenses from the cost of security to insurance.[10]

6. *We are most safe and most secure when we are most connected.* The willingness of neighbours to look after one another, and to actually intervene to protect one another when someone causes trouble, can reduce all kinds of crime in a neighbourhood. A local neighbourhood watch can reduce graffiti, muggings, even gang violence.[11]

§

I am part of a community workers' co-operative called the Community Praxis Co-op. The Co-op exists to empower people and resource and strengthen the capacities of groups and organizations in order to develop just, peaceful and sustainable communities. It undertakes projects in teams of two or more members, and the Co-op member I have done the most work with in a team is a brilliant community development practitioner by the name of Peter Westoby. In the car on the way to and from our Co-op work on government sponsored community development projects, Pete and I have had many long and vigorous talks about the art of community development.

Pete believes that community development is much less about technique, and more about soul, and that community development practitioners cannot simply move in and quickly mobilise a community to solve their own problems. According to Pete, we can only participate along with others in the community in invoking the 'soul of the community'. He often cites a quote from the mystic, Thomas Moore, who says that 'human community [is] the work of the ghosts of memory, the spirits of place and the soul of culture.'[12] Pete says that 'true community can only be born if there is some transformation of awareness and attention'. Community as a reality 'can only be dreamt of' when we are in touch with 'the archetypal mysteries of our psyches' in the depth of our souls. He says that we need 'models, images and pictures that enable us to imagine a new world' and can 'inspire a hope that ignites possibilities that seem beyond reality.'[13]

If we are going to enable one another to imagine a society with a greater sense of community, both Pete and I believe there are four things that we need to do. Firstly, we need to help one another recognise our hopes for the world, which usually involve some kind of renewal of community in our society. Secondly, we need to provide one another with an opportunity to explore alternative approaches to the renewal of community. These include those commended by the archetypal metaphors embedded in our psyches that are expounded in the mysteries of the major religious traditions. Thirdly, we need to establish places for substantive conversations — around those metaphors — about the possibilities of developing a renewed sense of significance and solidarity in society. Fourthly, we need to encourage one another to engage the world in the light of the possibilities that those metaphors provide, so that we do our best to create as many gracious community spaces in society as we can, to embrace our fellow human beings in a 'strong-but-gentle undeniably-beautiful sense of belonging'.[14]

§

The archetypal metaphor of community I would like to offer you for your consideration in this process is the Trinity, as it is so poignantly depicted in Rublev's Icon, *The Holy Trinity*.

According to Baxter Kruger,

> The Trinity is the most beautiful doctrine of the Christian faith. But it has been disastrously neglected and forgotten, and when it is talked about, the discussion is dominated by those philosophical types that get caught up in all the technicalities and miss the main point of it all.[15]

The famous philosopher, Immanuel Kant, probably spoke for a lot of people when he said, 'even if one claims to understand it, the doctrine of the Trinity provides [us with] nothing, absolutely nothing, of practical value.' He said that we need to face the fact that it 'offers absolutely no guidance for conduct.'[16]

However, Leonardo Boff, the liberation theologian, spoke for millions of poor people in basic ecclesial communities around the world, when he said that the 'divine society' was their 'permanent utopia' — the true social program for any human society seeking participation, equity and equality.[17]

My hope is that *A Divine Society* will provide a practical theology of the Trinity you can use as an imaginative framework to work towards more community in society.

This book is dedicated to my children and to my children's children.

Dave Andrews
Brisbane 2008

'The Secret of the Universe
Is in the Heart of God.
The Secret of Heaven on Earth
Is in that Heart of Love.
Love that breathes Reality
Into our Sacred Dreams,
Stirs forgotten Memories,
And sets our Spirits free.'

from *Songs of Love and Justice* by Dave Andrews

'In our Heart of Hearts,
We hold the Hope most dearly;
We hold the Hope most dearly
　for Humanity:
That we will come to see
The Love that we all feel
Become so real
We'll be Community
Like the Holy Trinity.

And every now and then
We glimpse the fragile Beauty,
We glimpse the fragile Beauty
　of our Unity:
And sometimes we can see
The Love that we all feel
Become so real
We are like Family
Speaking Smiles and Kissing Tears:

Through dark Nights of Prayer,
Hard Days of Care.
Pitting Hope against Despair.'

from *Songs of Joy and Sorrow* by Dave Andrews

PART ONE

THE TRINITY AS AN ICON OF COMMUNITY

A. AN ICON OF COMMUNITY

When I am teaching groups about community, I often ask people what they know about the Trinity. Some say they have no idea what the Trinity is. Is the Trinity some sort of Divine Triad? Some say it's a Christian idea of God — as 'Father, Son and Spirit'. Some say they have heard of a Hindu Trinity as well as the Christian Trinity — 'Brahma, Vishnu and Shiva'. I then ask those who seem to have some idea about the Trinity to tell me what they think it is. Some say that they think the Trinity is 'one God in three'. And some say the Trinity is 'three Gods in one'.

I then ask them to tell me how they explain the concept of the Trinity to themselves and to other people who might ask them about it. People brought up in the church will cite the classic Irish Catholic analogy of a 'shamrock' — 'one-leaf-in-three' and 'three-leaves-in-one'. Some of the more mathematically inclined people will say that while '1+1+1=3', it's also true that '1x1x1=1!' Sooner or later, one of the more scientifically inclined people will say that the Trinity, like H2O, can be the 'one substance expressed in three states' — 'solid' like the Father, 'liquid' like the Son, and 'gas' like the Spirit.

At this point in a recent course, a young man said that as far as he was concerned, 'the Trinity is like a Big Mac!' To start with I could scarcely believe such a crass commercial analogy. But he carefully unpacked his Big Mac hamburger analogy of the Trinity for us by saying:

> ...around the outside you've got the bun — like God the
> Father — that holds it all together; on the inside you've got
> the beef — like God the Son — who became flesh; and then,
> all through it, you've got the sauce — like God the Spirit —
> that gives it all its legendary flavour!

I think the laughter that greeted his analogy was probably a sign of the embarrassment people felt about using such a vulgar image for God. However, it was also probably a sign of relief that — at last! — someone had said something that we all could relate to.

The trouble is that most of our images of the Trinity are either not accessible or not accurate. On the one hand, the mathematical and the scientific models are simply not accessible to most people. On the other hand, the classic shamrock and funky Big Mac analogies are not accurate. They present the Trinity as impersonal and non-relational.

§

The most accessible and accurate picture of the Trinity that I have come across so far is a 14th century icon of the Trinity painted by Andrei Rublev, who lived between roughly 1360 and 1430. The painting is based on an Old Testament story from the Jewish Bible about the visit of three angels to Abraham and Sarah at Mamre (see Gen 18:1–15). According to traditional Orthodox theological interpretation of this passage, these angels were the three persons of the Trinity. Orthodox art scholars have always seen the icon as a picture of the perfect peaceful community, in stark contrast with the political conflict that was rife in Russia during the period when it was painted.

Orthodox Russians do not relate to icons as they would do to other paintings. They believe an icon is not a painting in the sense we normally regard pieces of art, although it is an image that is painted. Rather, it is a visual equivalent of Scripture, a window into the realm of God. Every paint stroke of an icon has a meaning hallowed by centuries of prayer. Not every religious painting is an icon, but an icon like The Holy Trinity is a religious painting that conveys the spiritual meaning of the subject matter.[18]

Before we go any further, let me confess that I feel very ambivalent about icons. I am Protestant, and one of the things that we Protestants have traditionally protested against is the use, or should I say the misuse, of icons. My wife is Greek Evangelical, but most of her relatives are Greek Orthodox, so many of the extended family weddings we go to are at the local Greek Orthodox Church. I always enjoy these weddings, except that every Protestant fibre in my body rebels against the idea of bowing to the priest and kissing the icon during the church service. However, having said that, I have found

Rublev's icon of *The Holy Trinity* so inspirational that I keep a replica of it in my study on the wall above my desk. The only time I take the icon down from its pride of place is when I take it — twice a year — as an exemplar for my session on the Trinity and community.

Rublev's Icon

When the Orthodox talk about an icon such as this, they tend to talk about the religious significance of the colours and the symbols.[19] They say things like:

> The colour blue is a symbol of heaven since the sky is blue and heaven is always considered to be 'up there'. All three figures are wearing blue and this indicates that all three figures must be heavenly beings.
> The colour gold is a symbol of wealth, riches and power. The figure on the left is wearing the most gold and therefore must be the most powerful. He must be the Father. The figure in the centre is also wearing a strip of gold on his right shoulder and therefore must share in this power. He must be the Son. Indeed, gold permeates the whole icon and gives it a strong and sumptuous feeling. The figure on the right must be the Spirit.
> The colour red is a symbol for blood. The figure in the centre is wearing red and therefore he must have some connection with blood or blood-shed. There is also red in the cup on the table. This is a piece of lamb.
> The colour green is a symbol of growth, new life, energy. The figure on the right is wearing green and so is associated with growth and new life.
> The house in the top left hand corner is the Father's house. Jesus said 'There are many rooms in my fathers house'. It is a symbol of heaven.
> The tree is close to the central figure, who is the Son, and it symbolizes the wood of the cross that he died on — which becomes the tree of life.
> The hill on the top right hand corner is a symbol of our

meeting place with God. These mountaintop experiences are associated with the Spirit.

The figures look more like women than men. They wear robes, have long hair and seem to have a hair tie on their heads. The artist is trying to tell us about the dual (masculine and feminine) nature of God (Gen 1:27).

The sticks are sceptres. They symbolize authority. A king would normally pronounce judgment with a sceptre in hand. All three figures hold a sceptre in their hand — indicating all three figures have equal authority.

The chalice on the table is a symbol of communion and fellowship. We are invited to eat and drink, to become part of this meal, this community.

When I show Rublev's icon to my group, I encourage them to talk about the non-religious, rather than religious, significance of the icon. I don't tell them anything about the traditional Orthodox interpretations of the colours and the symbols. I simply ask the participants to sit with the icon for a while and meditate on the image and its meaning for them. And finally I ask them to imagine what the icon might say to them about the Trinity as a community — and about the Trinity as a model for community development.

When they talk to me about what the icon says to them about the Trinity as a community, people say:

> The icon shows the Trinity as persons — not phantoms — but persons.
> Yeah. Real persons. But with funny kinds of bubbles on their heads.
> Those bubbles are haloes. Like auras. They show they're holy.
> The wings they all have depict their ability to fly way above the earth.
> But the staffs indicate their readiness to walk beside us on the road.
> There's three of them. I don't know why. But there's three of them.

> At a glance they all look the same, but they're all dressed differently.
> They look more like women than men. They even dress like women.
> That's classic male clothing, mate. But they look a bit metro-sexual.
> It seems like one in the middle is higher than the others, but he isn't.
> The other two look like they are lower, but they're on the same level.
> They all seem to be sitting around the table listening to one another.
> And in the middle is a dish of something or other that they're sharing.

When they talk to me about what the icon says to them about the Trinity as a model for community development, people say:

> The Trinity shows community as 'persons in relation to one another'.
> The haloes suggest that community won't work without a spirituality.
> Not just any spirituality — a healthy, holistic, holy spirituality of love.
> The Trinity shows there needs to be at least three to be community.
> Three seems to be a minimum. But there's room at the table for more.
> The icon shows that godly community includes both unity and diversity.
> It shows that godly community involves both masculinity and femininity.
> It also shows godly community entails equality — rather than hierarchy.
> The hill, the tree, and the house indicate real community is grounded.

> Sitting in a circle round the table depicts true community
> as hospitality.
> Each person in the circle is looking at and listening to
> the next person.
> The way they are sitting is open — not closed — inclusive
> and attentive.
> The mood suggests community involves sharing sorrow
> as well as joy.
> The cup of wine is a symbol of suffering at the heart
> of community.

Apart from the different interpretations of the contents of the chalice, both the religious and non-religious interpretations are essentially the same. In fact, if you argue that whether the content of the chalice is a piece of lamb or a cup of wine, it makes no difference — because both symbolize suffering — then you could say the religious and non-religious interpretations are exactly the same.

However, the trouble with the religious interpretations of the Trinity is they are so frightfully religious that they tend to scare off people who are not religious. To ensure that all people — non-religious as well as religious — can feel comfortable approaching the Trinity and exploring it as a classic spiritual metaphor for community and an innovative spiritual framework for community development, I always try to stay with the non-religious interpretations as much as possible.

§

The Holy Trinity is a picture of the ultimate reality of God as three persons in one community, devoted to love and justice, living in harmony for all eternity.

If what the icon is suggesting is true, it means, at the very least, *that the ultimate reality in the universe is not impersonal, but personal.* God is not chance 'playing dice with the universe'. Rather, *God is a community of three persons living in communion with one another and the world they have made.*

B. THE TRINITY AS PERSONS

*The icon shows the Trinity as persons —
not phantoms, but persons*

A person is a distinct identity who possesses the capacity to think, to feel and to act.[20] If we look at the icon we can see there are three distinct identities. They are not the same as one another, although they are very similar. Each has the capacity to think, to feel and to act — and to reflect on their actions and their interactions. 'Reason' — or the capacity to think — is the capacity to behave consciously in terms of the 'nature' of reality — in terms of the nature of what is really there. 'Emotion' — or the capacity to feel — is the capacity to behave consciously in terms of the 'value' of reality — in terms of the value of what is really there. Both reason and emotion are inextricably interconnected. There can be no 'objectivity about truth' unless there is 'subjectivity that is open to the truth'.[21] Attitudes to the truth will always affect ideas about truth. 'Morality' — or the expectation to act appropriately in terms of the nature and the value of things as they really are — is a product of reason and emotion. 'Duty' tends to emphasise 'principle' (based on reason) over 'passion' (based on emotion). 'Sincerity' tends to emphasise 'passion' (based on emotion) over 'principle' (based on reason). Persons with the 'sensibility' depicted in Rublev's icon combine both reason and emotion.

God is 'not a divine abstraction, a faceless, nameless, infinite, austere omni-being with no real personality'.[22] God personifies passionate and principled sensibility to such an extent that the best thing you can say about God is that 'God is love!' This means that no one should be afraid of God, for God's 'perfect love casts out fear' (1 Jn 4:16–18).

If the ultimate reality of the universe is a community of persons depicted in the Trinity, then we can trust that *the context in which we live is located in a community who think reasonably, feel emotionally and act morally with real sensibility!* I know it sounds too good to be true. But that's exactly why these views are called the 'Good News'.

C. THE TRINITY AS PERSONS IN RELATION

The Trinity shows community as
'persons in relation to one another'

A person is always a distinct identity in relation to another, at once subject and object. As a 'subject' he or she is an 'I'; as an 'object' he or she is 'You'. In science, other persons tend to be treated as 'means', or as objects of efficiency. In art, other persons tend to be treated as 'ends', or as objects of beauty. However, in the Trinity others are treated as 'friends' — not just as objects, but as other subjects — other selves, like 'ourselves', with whom one can create community that is well and truly reciprocal.[23]

Contrary to what much of our theology would lead us to believe, 'God is not an isolated sovereign, a self-centred king who demands that everything revolve around him. God is a circle of passion and life and fellowship.'[24] If we look at the icon we can see that each one in the Trinity is not only aware of the other, but also attentive to the other. The figure on the left has a hand raised — in blessing? — to the figure in the middle. The figure in the middle has a hand extended — in greeting? — to the figure on the right. And the figure on the right has a hand lowered — in deference? — to the figure on the left.[25]

The Jewish mystic philosopher, Martin Buber, has said that the spirituality of community simply consists of always treating 'the Other' as a 'Thou' — or a 'You' — rather than an 'It'. An economy may function on 'I-It' relationships, but a community can only function on 'I-You' relationships.[26] And all 'communities are based on two foundations, both of which reinforce these relationships. First, communities provide affective bonds that resemble extended families. Second, they transmit a moral framework...[for developing] extended families.'[27] So it is not surprising that the Trinity resembles an 'extended family' to such an extent that one person in the Trinity is said to love like a 'father' (see Mt 7:11) and another person in the Trinity is said to love like a 'mother' (see Lk 13:34). The moral framework they use to develop their extended family as a community is the simple rule of general reciprocity — to love others as you love yourself (see Mk 12:31).

Because the ultimate reality of the universe, as depicted in the Trinity, is a community of persons in relation to one another, we know that *being 'family' is fundamental to who we are — and we cannot become the family we are meant to be without keeping the family rule and loving others as we love ourselves.*

D. THE TRINITY AS THREE IN ONE

The Trinity shows there needs to be 'at least three to be community'

It takes *one* person to be an individual. It takes *two* people to make a couple. And it takes at least *three* people to make a community. I like to use the English word 'trey', derived from the French word 'trei' meaning 'three', as a simple, short memorable word for the 'threesome' we are talking about that creates an exponential explosion in potential — not only in the quantity, but also the quality — of relationships. A trey creates the possibility for people to go beyond personal interest. It is, they say, the beginning of a sense of common cause — a collective purpose — beyond what suits individual interests.[28] A trey creates the *stability* and *security* that is essential for community. If the relationship between two people is strained, in a threesome the relationship that the two people have with the third can hold the community together. As the ancient sage says: 'A threefold cord is not easily broken' (Eccl 4:12). A trey creates the subjectivity and objectivity essential for community. If there is a problem in a relationship between two people, in a threesome the problem can be understood *subjectively* by each of the two people involved and understood *objectively* by the third person, who can act as a witness. And it's common sense to decide on the 'evidence of two or three witnesses' (Mt 18:16). Finally — yet importantly — a trey creates the possibility for God to 'be love'. Love is a relationship between people that requires the individuality of one, the reciprocity of two, and the stability, subjectivity and objectivity of three. If God was just an individual, s/he could *'act with love'*, but could not 'be love'. If God was a couple, they could *'be in love'* and *'be loving'* — but could not actually *'be love'*. It is only because God is a community of Three-In-One that God can *'be love'* (1 Jn 4:8).

Because the ultimate reality of the universe, depicted in the Trinity, is a community of persons in relation to one another, we know the trey is the only way it is possible for people to relate to one another with the *individuality* of one, the *reciprocity* of two, and the *stability, subjectivity* and *objectivity* of three.

E. GENDER EQUITY IN THE TRINITY

They look more like women than men —
they even dress like women.
That's classic male clothing, mate.
But they look a bit metro-sexual.
It shows godly community involves
both masculinity and femininity.

Some people argue that, as the Trinity is dominated by a 'Father' figure, the community of God is a patriarchy in which the male dominates the female.

There is no doubt that, in the scriptures, each person in the Trinity has been given a patriarchal name rather than a matriarchal name; However, as the icon illustrates, each person in the Trinity demonstrates both masculine and feminine qualities, that in practice create gender equity in their community.

We can no more change the fact that Jesus called the first person in the Trinity 'Father,' rather than 'Mother', 'than we can decree he was not Jewish, or a wandering rabbi, or unpopular with the Sanhedrin.'[29] The patriarchal name is central to the Christian tradition. However, 'the reason the word "Father" is indispensable is not because there is any gender [bias] in God, but simply the givenness of the fact that Jesus used it in prayer' — most famously in The Lord's Prayer. While the name 'Father' is an important metaphor for God, it doesn't exclude other important metaphors like 'Mother.'[30] Indeed, even in Deuteronomy, the fifth book of the Pentateuch, the writer uses both masculine and feminine metaphors for God, when he says to the people of Israel, that God 'sired you [like a father], and God gave you birth [like a mother]' (see Deut 32:18). According to Genesis, the Spirit 'brooded' over the cosmos in creation, like a mother hen, sitting carefully on her clutch of eggs, waiting for them to hatch! (Gen 1:2). And according to the Gospels, when Christ comes, he picks up the same matriarchal rather than patriarchal theme, when he says, 'how often have I desired to gather your children together as a hen gathers her brood under her wings' (Mt 23:37). No wonder Rublev represents the Trinity as a meeting of the Mothers' Union! I agree with Latin American theologian, Leonardo Boff, who says that when we talk about God, we are talking about a maternal God-Father and a paternal God-Mother, so we need to feel free to use the pronoun 'He' when the metaphor used to refer to a figure is masculine — like 'Father' — and 'She' when the metaphor used to refer to a figure is feminine — like 'Mother.'[31]

The ultimate reality of the universe, depicted in the Trinity, is a community that *involves masculinity and femininity equally,* so we know that even though we may be confused about the meaning of these categories, there must be something of fundamental significance about gender and gender equity in community.

F. GENUINE EQUALITY IN THE TRINITY

It seems like one in the middle is
higher than the others, but he isn't.
The other two look like they are lower,
but they're on the same level.
It shows that godly community entails
equality — rather than hierarchy.

Some people argue that the relationship that defines the Trinity is a

Father-Son relationship, so the community is really a hierarchy that is top-down.

There is no doubt that, in the scriptures, from time to time the Trinity does take on a top-down approach to serve a specific bottom-up purpose; however, as the icon illustrates, it is *mutuality*, not *hierarchy*, that is at the heart of the Trinity, and each person in the Trinity encourages genuine equality in the community.

It is important to note that the first person in the Trinity whom we refer to as the 'Father' was not always the Father in an eternal superordinate position, and the second person in the Trinity whom we refer to as the 'Son' was not always the Son in an eternal subordinate position. On the occasion of the incarnation, when the first person helped the second person take on flesh and blood and be born as a finite human being, the writer to the Hebrews records that the first person said to the second person, 'You are my Son; today I have begotten you...I will be his Father' (Heb 1:5). The 'Father receives his fatherhood through this act of sending forth the Son'.[32] This sending of one of the persons of the Trinity from the heavenly community into an earthly community as a finite being — who would naturally be 'poorer', or less powerful than any infinite being — was not a decision imposed by the first person as a 'superior' on the second person as a 'subordinate'. To the contrary, the Scripture suggests that the second person voluntarily chose to give up his infinite 'equality' with first person, in order to demonstrate his commitment to finite 'equality' among the human beings to whose community he came! As the apostle Paul says, 'Let the same mind be in you that was in Christ Jesus, who, though he was in the form of God, did not regard equality with God as something to be exploited, but emptied himself, taking the form of a slave, being born in human likeness' (Phil 2:6-7). Paul argues that although Christ 'was rich, yet for your sakes he became poor, so that by his poverty you might become rich' (2 Cor 8:9) — So that there might be equality! (see 2 Cor 8:13–15).

This dynamic interaction prevents us from conceiving of the Trinity revolving round an eternally superordinate Father and an eternally subordinate Son. The steps that each person takes seems to be more in keeping with the drum beat playing for a circle dance than orders coming from a chain of command. It is all about mutuality, not hierarchy — interdependence, not domination.[33] Any top-down approach in the direction of the dance is to serve the purpose of arranging human communities on the basis of equality from the bottom up.

The ultimate reality of the universe, depicted in the Trinity, is a community that is defined by *mutuality*, rather than by *hierarchy*, and by its commitment to *equality* for others as well as themselves, so we should consider rearranging our priorities, take some lessons, and learn the steps of the circle dance ourselves.

G. GRACIOUS INCLUSIVITY IN THE TRINITY

The Trinity shows there needs to be
at least three to be a community.
Three seems to be a minimum.
But there's room at the table for more.
The way they are sitting is open — not
closed — inclusive and attentive.

Some people argue that the Trinity is an exclusive club 'for members only' — a clique that includes 'Father', 'Son' and 'Spirit', and nobody — *nobody* — else.

There is no doubt that, in the scriptures, at times the Trinity seems like it's an exclusive club. But it isn't. In fact, as the icon illustrates, the Trinity is so inclusive that you might be forgiven for thinking the only thing excluded from the Trinity is 'exclusivity' itself. Each person in the Trinity embraces the other, and expects the other to extend the same gracious inclusivity towards others. In order to make clear the extent of the inclusivity that there is in the Trinity, Christ as the 'Son' spells it out for his disciples, by telling them: 'Whoever has seen me has seen the Father' (Jn 14:9); 'I am in the Father and the Father is in me' (Jn 14:11); 'The Father and I are one' (Jn 10:30). They are that tight and are that together. According to the great Trinitarian theologian, Jurgen Moltmann, 'the divine persons exist so intimately with, for, and in one another that they themselves constitute themselves in their unique, incomparable and complete union'.[34] However, in praying for his disciples, Christ says,

> I ask not only on behalf of these, but also on behalf of those who will believe in me through their word, that they may all be one. As you, Father, are in me and I am in you, may they also be in us, so that the world may believe that you have sent me. (Jn 17:20–21)

Did you get that? He is not only praying that all of us might have a sense of community the same as the Trinity, but also that we might become part of the Trinity and participate in that unique, incomparable and complete union ourselves. Jesus tells his disciples, 'I give you a new commandment, that you love one another. Just as I have loved you, you also should love one another' (Jn 13:34). Furthermore,

> You have heard that it was said, 'You shall love your neighbour and hate your enemy. But I say to you, Love your enemies and pray for those who persecute you, so that you may be children of your Father in heaven; for he makes his sun rise on the evil and on the good, and sends rain on the righteous and on the unrighteous. (Mt 5:43–45)

As Paul Fiddes puts it, God is not 'content to find dancing partners within the divine communion alone.' God's circle dance is not a closed circle, but open to others. The Creator invites the created to join the eternal festivities.[35] Baxter Kruger picks up this theme in *The Great Dance*:

The shared life of God is not about isolation. It is all about fellowship. And fellowship means that God is not a sad, lonely, depressed being. God is essentially very happy. The [Trinity] live in a fellowship of free-flowing togetherness and delight — a great dance of shared life that is rich and full, passionate and creative, good and beautiful...as an act of mind-boggling philanthropy, God chose to open the circle and share the great dance with us...[And so] the very life of the Triune God, the fellowship and communion, the eternal joy and glory of the Father, Son and Spirit have been given to us. The great dance is now ours, as much as God's.[36]

Rublev's icon shows that in the Trinity, *there is always room at the table for more*. And heaven will come on earth when 'people will come from east and west, from north and south, and will eat in the kingdom of God' (Lk 13:29).

PART TWO

A DIVINE MODEL FOR HUMAN COMMUNITY

*The colour blue is a symbol of heaven since the sky
is blue and heaven is always considered to be 'up
there'. All three figures in the icon are wearing blue and
this indicates all three figures are heavenly beings.*

The Trinity unveiled is a *heavenly* community involved with *earthly* society. Each of the Persons in the community are personally involved with society. Because of their complete interdependence, each one is implicated in the various roles each other plays in creating, liberating and sustaining society. However, each Person in the community chooses to play one particular role. The name that each of the Persons in the Trinity is called, tells us something about what role they choose to play and about how they choose to play it.

Traditionally the first person of the Trinity was called the 'Father' because he chose to play the role of a cosmic parent to all his children; the second Person of the Trinity was called the 'Son' because he chose to play the role of the 'model child' for all his brothers and sisters; and the third Person of the Trinity was called the 'Spirit' because s/he chose to play the role of the motivator. The names — Father, Son and Spirit — are metaphors, and not necessarily the best metaphors to use to speak of God in today's world. These names might have been helpful in pre-modern society, but they aren't so helpful in a post-modern society — especially a post-modern society committed to gender equity. Thus, I suggest we consider more appropriate names for each of the persons. Even if the words Father, Son and Holy Spirit are divinely inspired, that doesn't mean we need to use them any more than the Jews had to use the word 'Yahweh' — God's own name — which they habitually replaced with euphemisms such as 'Lord'.[37]

People have suggested many alternative names for the three persons in the Trinity:

The First Person	The Second Person	The Third Person
The Primordial One	The Expressive One	The Unitive One
Sine Qua Non	God Incarnate	God Incognito
Pathos	*Logos*	*Ethos*
Sat	*Chit*	*Ananda*
Creator	Liberator	Sustainer
The Truth From the Start	The Story At The Centre	The Experience In The End
The Reality Around us	The Flesh Beside us	The Breath Inside us
The Love that brings life to others	The Love that brings life with others	The Love that brings life out in others

Table 1: Suggested alternative names for the three Persons in the Trinity.

Primordial One, Expressive One and Unitive One don't do it for me.[38] I like the Greek — *Pathos*, *Logos* and *Ethos*, and Sanskrit — *Sat*, *Chit*, and *Ananda*. And I like Reality, Flesh and Breath even more.[39] However, I think Creator, Liberator and Sustainer are more personal, accurate and accessible terms.

When people relate to God, they generally tend to relate to one Person in the Trinity more than the others. Different people in different religions tend to relate to different Persons in the Trinity. Jews and Muslims tend to relate to God the Creator who is 'outside us'. Christians tend to relate to Christ the Liberator who is 'beside us'. Many Hindus and most Buddhists tend to relate to the Sustainer who is the Spirit 'inside us'.

Even within the same religion, different people will relate to different Persons of the Trinity. Within Christianity, liberals tend to relate to God best as Creator, stressing the importance of the preservation of creation, the promotion of peace and justice and the practice of spiritual, social, economic and environmental sustainability. Evangelicals tend to relate to God best as Liberator, stressing the importance of the incarnation of Christ, the preaching of the gospel of salvation, and the practice of personal and corporate transformation — being 'born again' and 'living life to the full'. Charismatics tend to relate to God best as Sustainer, stressing the importance of the experience of the Spirit, being 'baptised in the Spirit', and the practice of the 'gifts of the Spirit' and the 'fruit of the Spirit' in an dynamic, ongoing, life-changing way.

The trouble with these unitary — as opposed to Trinitarian — approaches to God is not in what they value, but in what they devalue. They value the role of one Person of the Trinity over and above — and sometimes over and against — the role of another Person in the Trinity. In the process, they devalue the role of another Person in the Trinity. As a Christian, I am painfully aware of how often Christians celebrate the role God has played in Christ over against the role God plays in creativity and spirituality, resulting in a tragic disregard for the roles God plays that are celebrated in other religions. As an evangelical — some might say post-evangelical — Christian, I am also acutely conscious of how often we evangelicals fail to learn what liberals, charismatics and others can teach us about the way God works in the world outside of the myopic focus of our own particular philosophical framework.[40]

So, let us explore *what* role each Person — Creator, Liberator and Sustainer — chooses to play and *how* they choose to play their roles with people in society — creating, liberating, and sustaining a heavenly kind of community on earth.

1. THE CREATOR

The wings they all have depict
their ability to fly way above the earth.
But the staffs indicate their readiness
to walk beside us on the road.
The colour gold is a symbol of riches, wealth and
power. The figure on the left is wearing the most
gold and must be extraordinarily powerful.

If we read Rublev's Icon according to tradition, from left to right, the first person on the left is the first person in the Trinity — the One we'll call the 'Creator'.

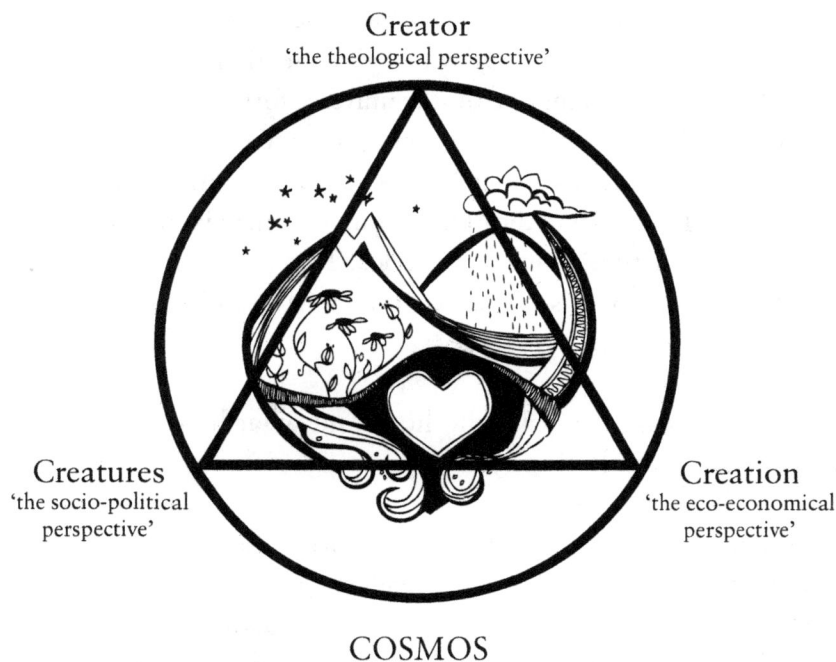

Figure 1: The Creator's role from multiple perspectives.

There are logically only three possible views of the relationship between the Creator and the cosmos. The first is that the Creator is identified with the cosmos and is in all aspects inseparable from it and all that exists. This is *pantheism*. The second is that the Creator is not identified with the cosmos and is in all aspects independent of it. This is *theism*. The third view is that the Creator is involved with the cosmos but is not identified with it. The relationship between the Creator, the creation and its creatures, is dynamic, interactive and interdependent. This is *panentheism*. Panentheism is also known as 'process theology' because reality is seen as a process God is personally involved with.[42] According to the latter view, the Creator's relationship with the creation involves an ethical framework that includes a *theological*, *eco-economic*, and *socio-political* perspective.[43]

A. The Theological Perspective

From a theological perspective, God designed the emerging universe in which we live.

> Everything alive is moving, even that which appears to stand still. Call it evolution if you will. Call it creation if you prefer. The engine that drives the universe forward is not natural selection but the dreaming of God. God's dreams pervade the world as a song haunts your mind; summoning, luring, calling. Where they find resonance, there is movement. God calls the tune; some of us dance. This waltz between God and the world is the source of all that is, and more importantly, what is yet to be.[44]

Love is God's essence, it is who he is and what he does. Of course, the word 'love' is itself sloppy.

> Teenagers are convinced the rush of hormones flooding their bodies is 'love'. The mindbenders have used it to sell chocolate and perfume. Love has been trivialised — like Bach played on a kazoo…[Nevertheless] genuine love exists. The river of love between two people is at its deepest point an intimation of the heart of God. [And] the heart of God has gone out from itself to envelope the universe. Love is the source of its existence, love the energy streaming through it, love the end to which it moves…God is the one who dreamed you into being, danced with joy at your birth [and] tracked you down the backstreets of your life, whispering to you in the night, calling you [back to your self] from the darkness.[45]

> Because God is love, and human beings are made in God's image, love is who we are. Love is not first and foremost something we do. It is who we are. Love is the essence of being human. To live is to let love well up and stream through us as the pulse of our lives, connecting us to ourselves, our neighbours, the whole family of earth's creatures, and God, the alpha and omega of love. To love is to be seeking, fostering and sustaining connections with that which is different and other — without domination, absorption or fusion — in delight, in care, in compassion.[46]

We are made by love for love. We love, therefore, we are.

§

Baxter Kruger says that,

> ...the very life of the Triune God is the invisible river running through our lives and through all things. The beauty of a given morning, the smile of a daughter saying everything that needs to be said, a cup of coffee with an old friend, the passion of love, the peace of fishing in the shadows of a dying day. It is poetry in motion being played out through the scenes of our lives...There are not two human races — one that is created by the Trinity, and another that is just human, ordinary, secular. There is only one human race, and that is the human race that has been drawn within the circle of the Trinity. There is therefore nothing ordinary at all about human existence...The human community is forever immersed in — and permeated by — the love of the divine community. Through creation 'we are genuine participants in the life of God.' Our problem is not that it is not so — it is we do not know that it is so.[47]

We are like the fish in a Sufi story who anxiously swim around looking for water — until they realise they are swimming in it. Once we realise that we are immersed in the 'river of God's providential love', we can learn to let go and float in it — putting our full weight on the water, trusting that we will always be supported. The confidence we need to have, in order to let go and float in the river of God's love, comes from letting God's love 'wash over us' and from 'soaking in the assurances of that love' which come our way every day.[48]

In the Judeo-Christian tradition, faith involves

> ...deep trust in the watchful love of God for all God's children. According to the prophet Isaiah, even in the midst of the most terrible circumstances, those whose hearts are centred

in God's faithful care 'shall renew their strength, they shall mount up on wings like eagles, they shall run and not be weary, they shall walk and not faint.'[49] (see Is 40:31)

According to David Benner,

> While human love can never bear the weight of our need for divine love, it can teach us about divine love. Human love can communicate divine love. Experiences of human love make the idea of God's love believable. The relative constancy of the love of family and friends makes the absolute faithfulness of divine love at least conceivable…[However, there is] no substitute for learning what love really is by coming back to the source. God's love is the original that shows up the limitations of all copies. Only God's love is capable of making us into great lovers.[50]

Wayne Muller observes that 'it is not the fact of being loved that is life changing. It is the experience of allowing [ourselves] to be loved.'[51] This experiential knowing of ourselves as deeply loved by God deepens our thoughts with new data about our world, and deepens our feelings with new attitudes towards our world. In the light of our knowledge of God's love, we know we can trust God, take risks and embrace the world that we live in courageously.

God's love connects us to all of God's creation and all of God's creatures. It moves us

> …from the isolation of self-interest to a connection with life that cannot allow any ultimate divisions. It does not allow [us] to limit [our] interest to those within [our] tribe — whether those tribal boundaries are understood in religious, ethnic or national terms…[Instead, it involves us in a] movement beyond the hardened boundaries of the isolated self to the selves-in-relationship that make up community [leading to] a sense of [our] oneness with all [life].[52]

B. The Eco-Economic Perspective

The 'eco-economic angle' of the Creator's involvement with the universe is best seen in the archetypal stories in Genesis, the very first book of the Bible, whose name means 'beginning'. The early chapters of book give us two distinct, but complementary, beautifully poetic accounts of the 'beginning'. The first is the macro-version in Genesis 1:1–2:3, which is followed by the micro-version in Genesis 2:4–25.

Both of these stories paint wonderful pictures. God is introduced as a Creator who takes the initiative, right from the start. Everything God does, from beginning to end, is 'good'. And God's goodness impregnates every single part of our universe, bringing our beautiful world to birth with great joy. God then creates us — men and women — equal, in God's image, as co-creators, to care for the world that was created. So men and women stand together at the beginning of history, 'naked and unashamed.'

Although I love these stories, I know other people hate them because of the way the texts have been used — or misused — to rationalise and sacralise terrible acts of economic imperialism and environmental vandalism. Yet if we study these texts carefully, we'll find a perfect prototype for economic responsibility and environmental sustainability.

In the macro-creation narrative, God is portrayed as creating everything. And each time God creates something, there is a cosmic shout that announces its presence and pronounces it 'good'. To the Creator, every thing created has intrinsic value and inherent worth. There is not one thing that should be treated as unimportant or insignificant.

According to process theology, every thing in creation is 'dipolar', with both a *mental* and a *physical* dimension, though at the lowest level of reality — such as subatomic particles — 'mind' has not yet reached 'consciousness' as it does in humans. These individual entities join to form collective societies which 'work together in the organic community of the world, influencing and being influenced by others, moving towards the achievement of beauty and value'.[53] God offers the 'parameters for development to every entity in creation to enable it to grow into fullness of life, and, because there is mental as well as physical element in everything, all can accept, reject or modify divine purpose.'⁵⁴

In Genesis, God is depicted as making humans 'from the dust of the ground'. As if to stress humanity's essential connectedness to the rest of the creation, we are also told that they were created on the same day as all the land-based animals — along with the sheep, cattle, horses, lions, tigers and chimpanzees.⁵⁵

However, Genesis not only presents the *continuities* God made between humanity, the 'ground', and other 'land-based creatures', it also presents the *discontinuities* God made between distinctly different parts of the created whole. In the original Hebrew text, the word translated 'created' is used only three times. The first time, it refers to the creation of 'the cosmos' (see Gen 1:1). The second time, it refers to the creation of 'consciousness' (see Gen 1:21). The third time, it refers to the creation of 'God-consciousness' (see Gen 1:27). Both creationists and evolutionists would see these as significant differences in the stages of the development of consciousness in the cosmos.⁵⁶

These narratives suggest that, while God created some significant *similarities* between humanity and the rest of the cosmos, God actually created very significant *differences* between humanity and the rest of the cosmos. Humanity, like other creatures, is conscious; however, unlike any other creature, humanity is uniquely *God-conscious*, because it was made by God, in the image of God, to manage creation on God's behalf (see Gen 1:26–27).

In these narratives it is clear that creation and its creatures do *not* belong to humanity. They belong to God. As the psalmist says in Psalm 24:1, 'The earth is the Lord's and all that is in it, the world, and those who live in it.' It is clear that humanity is not at liberty to do whatever it likes with 'the earth and everything it', because it 'is the Lord's'! On the contrary, humanity is expected to manage God's creation and God's creatures for God, on God's behalf.

§

How does God expect humanity to manage the earth and everything in it? In these, and other biblical accounts, the parameters are clearly spelled out in terms of four commands: *care for it, work with it, be fruitful* and *share it*. God's commands demand the economic responsibility and environmental sustainability that all humans know, deep down, constitute our obligation.

We are to *care for it*,

> as creatures who possess humanity, [we have] the cultural imperative to be caretakers, good neighbours to one another and to the other creatures...in taking care of our fellow creatures, we acknowledge that they are not ours; we acknowledge that they belong to an order and a harmony of which we ourselves are parts.[57]

We are also to *work with it*. In Wendell Berry's words, 'We cannot exempt ourselves from living in this world, and if we wish to live, we cannot exempt ourselves from using the world. If we cannot exempt ourselves from use, then we must deal with the issues raised by use in the context of care.'[58] He goes on to say that we can only use the world in the context of care where we live, as Adam and Eve did in the Garden of Eden, in a locality that we know and love. After all, 'people exploit what they value, but protect what they love.' If we are to protect creation and 'the world's multitudes of creatures', we must

> ...know them, not just conceptually, but imaginatively as well. They must be pictured in the mind; they must be known with affection, 'by heart', so that in remembering them the heart may be said to 'sing', to make music peculiar to its recognition of each particular creature that it knows well.[59]

However, we must acknowledge there is no completely harmless use of a place. Even the most basic use of a place as a source of sustenance causes some degree of harm. 'Even the most scrupulous vegetarian must eat food that would otherwise be eaten by other creatures. So by the standard of absolute harmlessness, the two available parties are not vegetarians and non-vegetarians, but rather eaters and non-eaters.' The challenge is to reduce the hurt caused in harm to a minimal irreducible level. And, one of the first things God does to reduce hurt, is to circumscribe the use of animals for food and instead recommend 'every green plant for food'.[60]

We are to *be fruitful* in our work. There is an expectation of growth, but it is of organic growth — healthy, holy, sustainable growth.

> In a viable neighbourhood, neighbours ask themselves what they can do for one another, and they find answers that they and their place can afford. This, and nothing else, is the practice of neighbourhood. This practice must be, in part, charitable, but it must also be economic, and the economic part must be equitable[61]…A viable community is made up of neighbours who cherish and protect what they have in common. This is the principle of subsistence. It does not import products it can produce for itself. It does not export products until local needs have been met.[62]

The fruit of our labour is not only for ourselves; it is to be *shared* with others. We are constantly reminded of where our desire should lie in this respect:

> Is it not to share your bread with the hungry, and bring the homeless poor into your house; when you see the naked, to cover them, and not to hide yourself from your own kin? (Is 58:7)

> I do not mean that there should be relief for others and pressure on you, but it is a question of a fair balance between your present abundance and their need, so that their abundance may be for your need, in order that there may be a fair balance. (2 Cor 8:13–15)

§

When God created humanity, he created men and women with the capacity to *choose* to cooperate with Gods proposals, or to repudiate Gods plans. God does not manipulate people's choices, but seeks to persuade people 'by haunting the soul with the pressure of [the] unconditional value' of the proposals.[63] Theologian Paul Fiddes states that in God's proposals, 'God provides aims to guide all entities in the world on their path towards [their] satisfaction, though they are free to [accept,] to reject, or to modify them.'[64]

The archetypal story about choice — about whether to accept or reject God's proposals for our lives — is the story of the temptation in the Garden of Eden, where the choice is set out in Genesis 3:1–13 and the consequences in Genesis 4:1–17.

God told Adam and Eve, 'You may freely eat of every tree of the garden; but of the tree of the knowledge of good and evil you shall not eat, for in the day that you eat of it you shall die' (Gen 2:16–17). They were free to do what they liked — as long as they were prepared to live their lives within the ethical framework the Creator had set for them. The only thing that Adam and Eve needed to keep in mind was to recognize the limitations of their knowledge, to continue to depend on God for their knowledge of good and evil, and not try to access the knowledge of good and evil independently of God.

Now, if you think about it, the Creator's requirement is not unreasonable. After all, what options do human beings have to decide about the good or evil of a particular action? One option is tradition. But they had no tradition. Another option is Scripture. But they had no Scripture. Another option includes practising virtues. But who decides which virtues are the most appropriate to act on at a particular time and place? Other options include the 'consequentialist' approach, which seeks to choose an action that has the best consequences; or the 'utilitarian' approach, which seeks to do the greatest good for the greatest number; or the 'categorical imperative' approach, which seeks to make sure that anything done would be universally acceptable to everyone. All of which are commendable ethical approaches. However, who is in a position to know what action will produce the best consequences, the greatest good for the greatest number, and the universally acceptable to everyone — except God, who is the only one in a position to know all the possible consequences of a choice?

As our drama unfolds, a 'snake in the grass' appears unexpectedly in paradise. And its sudden unexplained appearance changes everything in paradise forever. The snake asks Adam and Eve the ultimate religious question: 'Did God say?' 'Did God say "you are free to eat from any tree in the garden; but you must not eat from the tree of the knowledge of good and evil, for when you eat of it you will surely die"?' (see Gen 3:1–4). Only, as Adam and Eve talk with the snake about it, what God says is subtly changed, so in the end, it sounds anything *but* reasonable!

The snake subtracts a little from what God says. It leaves out the bit about all the stuff God says they *can freely eat*, and only leaves in the stuff about what God says they *can't eat*. Eve picks up on the snake's insinuation about God's restrictiveness and emphasizes it by adding a little to what God says herself. She says God says they will be in trouble even if they just so much as *touch* the forbidden fruit. As Eve listens to what she says God says, it must sound terribly unreasonable to her. And no self-respecting human being has ever been willing to subordinate himself or herself to an unreasonable demand. She is ready to rebel, but hesitates in fear of the consequences — until the snake tells her, 'God says you will die. But I tell you, you will not die. The only reason God is threatening you, is because God knows when you eat of the forbidden fruit your eyes will be opened and you will be like God, knowing good and evil'. Like any of us in the same situation, Eve considers the choice before her: to continue to subordinate herself to an unjust God, or to become her own God.

Tempted, Eve considers the forbidden fruit, sees that it looks extraordinarily beautiful and delicious and is 'desirable for gaining wisdom' — and goes for it.

Once Adam and Eve acted unilaterally, without reference to anyone but themselves, their 'eyes were opened' and they saw reality in a new light. They weren't in a better position to know any more about good and evil philosophically; but they were in a position to know more about good and evil personally. When they had collaborated with the Creator in taking care of the creation, Adam and Eve had known the delight of what it was like to do good. Now that they had acted unilaterally, without any reference to anyone but themselves, Adam and Eve knew the distress of what it was like to do bad. Too late, they realised that they had made a big mistake. They felt embarrassed, ran away and hid. When they were found out, they did what most of us would do in the same situation: they blamed everyone else but themselves. And, in scapegoating others, Adam and Eve knew the terrible indignity of what it was like to do evil.

However, Adam and Eve did not 'die'. They lived on, and went on to have children, one of whom built a city — the foundation of modern civilisation as we know it. Only, according to the Hebrews — for whom *maveth*, their word for 'death', means 'disconnection' — Adam and Eve did 'die' that day they disconnected from God. And their son Cain built modern civilisation on a culture of 'death'. Without God we not only lose our way, but we also lose any idea of how we can find our way again. At our best, we acknowledge our mistake. At our worst, we kill one another as 'scapegoats'. We build environments, which exclude the natural wonders that remind us of a God whom we prefer to forget, and economies that disregard the call to be our 'brother or sister's keepers'.

§

Whenever humanity disconnects with God, we lose our way. The existentialist philosopher, Jean Paul Sartre, is forced to admit painfully that, 'there disappears with [God], all possibility of finding values in an intelligible heaven.'[65]

Too late, we realise God's guidelines are not good because they are recommended, but are recommended because they are *necessary* for unity and harmony.[66] Too late, we realise disregarding God's guidelines is not evil because it is forbidden, but it is forbidden because disregarding God's guidelines *divides us* from our neighbours and the world.[67] The anti-Nazi activist-theologian, Dietrich Bonhoeffer, wrote that when we choose the tree of life, we choose intimate relational dependence on God where all is 'infused with the sacred', and 'saturated with love'. This is the *ontology of life*, which is grounded in God who is the origin and destiny of creation. According to Bonhoeffer, 'This life cannot know death'. However, when we choose the tree of the knowledge of good and evil, we choose autonomy from God, we separate ourselves from the 'essence of sacred' and the 'source of love'. This is the *ontology of death* which is grounded in alienation from God, whose sacred heart of love is the origin and destiny of creation. 'This life cannot know life.'[68]

Too late, we realise we have substituted curiosity and control for our duty of care. Too late, we realise that 'curiosity is an amoral passion, a need to know that allows no guidance beyond the need itself.' Too late, we realise that 'control is simply another word for power, a passion notorious not only for its amorality but for its tendency toward corruption. If curiosity and control are the primary motives for our knowing, we will generate a knowledge that eventually carries us not toward life but death.' Too late, we realise that 'curiosity sometimes kills, and our desire for control has put deadly power in some very unsteady hands'. We should not be surprised that 'knowledge launched from these sources is heading toward some terrible ends, undeflected by ethical values as basic as respect for life itself.'[69]

Too late, we realise we have opted for materialistic values — what looks beautiful and delicious and desirable — at the expense of non-materialistic values, such as caring for the earth and sharing the wealth we have with others. The more materialistic we are, the less likely we are to share our wealth. In 2002 there was a major independent review of aid, which showed that while the wealth per person in donor countries had doubled since 1961, the aid given per person had decreased. These days Australians give 0.25 percent of gross national product in aid, and Americans give a paltry 0.1 percent in humanitarian aid! It seems the more greedy we become, the more uncaring even the most caring among us become. In her book *Caring*, Nel Noddings argues that we only have an obligation to care for our own. She maintains that we are 'not obliged to care for starving children in Africa!'[70] And consequently starving children in Africa and elsewhere die every day from treatable causes because we refuse to share.

The more materialistic we are, the less likely we are to care for the earth, even though we all know that it is the only source we have for our wealth. The current pattern of material consumption is environmentally unsustainable. In Clive Hamilton's words, 'Cities with millions of high-consumption residents act like huge vacuum cleaners, sucking in resources and then blowing out huge volumes of wastes that must be buried, dumped into the oceans, or vented into the atmosphere.'[71] Hamilton cites following statistics: It takes the biosphere 'at least a year and three months to renew what humanity uses in a single year, so humanity is now eating into earth's natural capital'; each person in the US requires '10.3 hectares of land to meet their consumption needs and absorb their waste products — this compares with "footprints" of 0.8 hectares in India and a [global)] availability of land of 1.7 hectares per person'; 'If everyone in the world were to consume as much as the average consumer in the rich countries we would require four planets the size of earth!'[72]

§

The Creator directly challenges the development of a single centralised political economy that disregards the call to be our 'brother or sister's keepers'. We see this in the account of the rise and fall of the Tower of Babel in Genesis 11:1–9. This tower is the archetypal example of human hubris: 'Come, let us build ourselves a city, and a tower with its top in the heavens, and let us make a name for ourselves; otherwise we shall be scattered abroad upon the face of the whole earth' (Gen 11:4). It is a symbol of a spiritually defiant, self-referenced, other-controlling diabolical creativity which shows no sensitivity towards creation itself. It asserts its autonomy — void of morality — on the basis of adept technology. It is no wonder that JRR Tolkien drew on this symbolism when writing of 'the dark tower' in *The Lord of the Rings*.[73]

Many no doubt saw the World Trade Towers in New York as modern equivalents, symbolizing the power of the global political economy centred inequitably in the USA. And — as we have seen before our very eyes — forces from within globalization inevitably tear down the 'tower of global utopia' founded on injustice, and reduce us to 'parochial anarchy' that makes the possibility of global civilization an unattainable aspiration in the present circumstances.[74]

The Creator seeks to ensure the survival of creation by proposing a couple of 'covenants'. He made an everlasting covenant with Noah and every living creature, and symbolized it by the sign of a rainbow in the sky (see Gen 9:12–16). He made another covenant with Abraham and Sarah, assuring them that he would 'bless' them — and through them — would bless 'all the peoples on earth' (see Gen 12:1–2; 17:15–16).

C. The Socio-Political Perspective

The 'socio-political angle' of the Creator's involvement with the universe is also best seen in some of the archetypal stories in the early books of the Bible.

Rabbi Jonathan Sacks says that we need to go back to Genesis to re-discover *The Politics of Hope*. He says,

> In its initial verses...the Bible sets out two propositions that will frame its entire vision of mankind. The first affirms the sanctity of the human individual as individual. Every person is in 'the image of God'. The second asserts the incompleteness of the individual as individual. 'It is not good for man (sic) to be alone.' Hence the human need for relationship, association, and for stable structures within which these can grow and be sustained...[75]

The Rabbi then goes on to ask and answer a key question. 'How do we move from unbearable isolation to some form of tolerable association? By way of answer, I want to tell two stories both implicit in the Bible, but quite different in their implications...'[76]

The first story the Rabbi tells is the *political story* most famously told by Thomas Hobbes in *The Leviathan* (1651). The Rabbi says that Hobbes starts with what he calls the 'state of nature'; which the Rabbi says is very close to the biblical description of the state of post-fall 'unmediated conflict' just before the Flood. In this state of 'unmediated conflict', Hobbes says, people are 'in that condition which is called "War"; and such a war as is of every man, against every man (sic)'. The outcome of which, Hobbes says, is that life is inevitably 'solitary, poor, nasty, brutish, and short'.

The Rabbi asks 'How then do human beings create societies which can ensure a degree of security and safety?' The Rabbi says that Hobbes' answer to this question is: that in order protect ourselves from the pre-emptive attacks of others, we 'hand over some of our powers as individuals to a supreme authority which will make laws and enforce them'. This, the Rabbi says, is the origin of the 'social contract', which 'brings into being the "great Leviathan" of the state, and thus is born *political society*...needed to bring about a order'.

According to the *political story*, associations are created to 'contain conflict by the use of external power, by legislation or taxation backed up, in extremis, by the threat of coercive force — an army or police force'. For Hobbes, the use of force is the foundation of society.[77]

The second story the Rabbi tells is a *social story* which he says 'begins at the same starting-point, but using different concepts and evoking a distinct set of themes. The simplest way of proceeding is to ask what actually happens in the Hebrew Bible after the words: 'It is not good for man [sic] to be alone'? God creates woman. Man then responds with the first poem in the Bible:

> This is now
> bone of my bone,
> flesh of my flesh;
> she shall be called woman *[ishah]*
> because she was taken from man *[ish]*. (Gen 2:23)'

The Rabbi insists on using two Hebrew words, because, 'the Hebrew text contains a nuance often missed in translation. Until this point man (sic) has been called *adam*, man-as-part-of-nature (the word *adam* signifies 'that which is taken from the earth'). Now for the first time man (sic) is called — indeed calls himself — *ish*, which means man-as-person. Significantly, he does this only after he has named woman. The Bible is suggesting, with great subtlety, that the human person must first pronounce the name of the other before he can know his own name. He or she must say "Thou" before he can say "I". Relationship precedes identity.'

According to the Rabbi, in this spiritual story 'the primary social bond is not the state, but marriage' ('Therefore a man will leave his father and mother and be united to his wife, and they will become one flesh', Genesis 2:24). What kind of bond is this? Clearly, given the way the Hebrew Bible describes it, it is not a Hobbesian contract between two independent individuals, each seeking their own interests. It is instead — in a key word of Jewish thought — a covenant (*brit* in Hebrew), and this is neither an alliance of interests nor, strictly speaking, an emotional state. Instead it is a bond of identity, as if to say: 'This is part of who I am'.

> This central concept is taken up in various ways in the Hebrew Bible. There is a covenant handed on by parents and children (the subject of much of Genesis) and another and more structured covenant at Mount Sinai, with the Israelites as a people. This affects the way the Bible understands certain obligations. Consider welfare. The book of Leviticus defines the duties of citizens to one another with such phrases as 'If your brother becomes poor'. On this view, I owe help to others, not because it is in my long term interest to do so, nor because a government has so decreed, but because the other is part of my extended family, and thus in a certain sense part of who I am. The members of a society are linked by a bond of kinship and fraternity.[78]

What is the difference between the *political* and the *social* stories the Rabbi tells?

The first distinctive the Rabbi points out is that in the *political* story the central figure is 'I', whereas in the *social* story the central figure is 'We'. In the *political* story, my association with others is not essential, but a necessary evil I need to construct in order to ensure my survival. In the *social* story, our affiliation with one another is essential, and is inherently good. 'The "We" of which "I" am a part — marriage, the family, the nation (is) understood as an extended family, and ultimately humanity itself, considered as a single family under the parenthood of God himself.'

The second distinctive the Rabbi points out is that in the *political* story the driving force behind my actions is self interest, whereas in the *social* story the driving force behind our interactions is identification with others. Our 'responsibilities flow from belonging' — 'the kind of relationship that exists between husbands and wives, or parents and children.' The bible refers to this kind of relationship as *"hesed"*, which is usually translated "compassion".'[79]

The third distinctive the Rabbi points out is that in the *political* story the dominant form of association is a contract, whereas in the *social* story the dominant form of affiliation is a covenant (*brit*). People who make contracts are bound to fulfil the letter of the law on which they are based. People who make covenants are bound to go beyond the letter of the law to fulfil the love for one another on which they are based.'Parties can disengage from a contract when it is no longer to their mutual benefit to continue. A covenant binds them even — perhaps especially — in difficult times. This is because a covenant is not predicated on interest, but instead on loyalty, fidelity, holding together even when things seem to be driving you apart.' The Rabbi says that a covenants has a 'moral component that renders them more binding and open-ended than could be accounted for in terms of interest.' So much so that the Hebrew word *"hesed"*, which is usually translated "compassion", might be more accurately translated as 'covenantal obligation'.[80] Daniel Elazar says that the idea of covenant 'expresses the idea that people can freely create communities and polities, peoples and publics, and civil society itself through such morally grounded and sustained compacts (whether religious or otherwise in impetus), establishing thereby enduring partnerships'.[81]

The fourth distinctive the Rabbi points out is that in the *political* story the contract is maintained by the threat and the use of force, whereas in the *social* story the covenant is maintained by faithfulness (*emunah*). 'A contract is maintained by an external force, the monopoly within the state of the justified use of coercive power. A covenant, by contrast, is maintained by an internalised sense of identity, loyalty, obligation, responsibility and reciprocity.' "*Emunah*" is at the heart of the Jewish religion. It is often wrongly translated as 'faith'. However, *emunah* is not an 'intellectual attribute' but a 'moral one'. It does not mean 'faith'. It means 'faithfulness' 'It signifies the willingness to enter into and to stand by a long-term, open-ended commitment. It is what is needed to sustain a covenant'.[82]

So, the Rabbi says,

> there are two stories about human associations, one told in our political classics, the other in our great religious texts. A contract (advocated in our political classics) gives rise to the instrumentalities of the state — governments, nations, parties, the use of centralised power and the mediated resolution of conflict. It is the basis of political society. A covenant (advocated in our great religious texts) gives rise to quite different institutions — families, communities, peoples, traditions, and voluntary associations. It is the basis of civil society.'[83]

2. THE LIBERATOR

The mood suggests community involves
sharing sorrow as well as joy.
The cup of wine is a symbol of
the suffering at the heart of community.
The colour red is a symbol for blood.
The figure in the centre is wearing red
and therefore must have some sort of
connection with bloodshed

If we again read Rublev's icon according to tradition, from left to right, the second person from the left is the second Person in the Trinity — the One we'll call the 'Liberator'.

Whereas the Creator is a mystery who is all around us — above and below us — but beyond us, the Liberator is the invisible made visible in flesh and blood — who actually comes alongside us and battles for our liberation as one of us.

In Jesus of Nazareth — whom we know as the 'Messiah' or the

'Christ' — God demonstrates a life of radical non-violent sacrificial *compassion*, which is the only way of life that can save us from destroying ourselves.

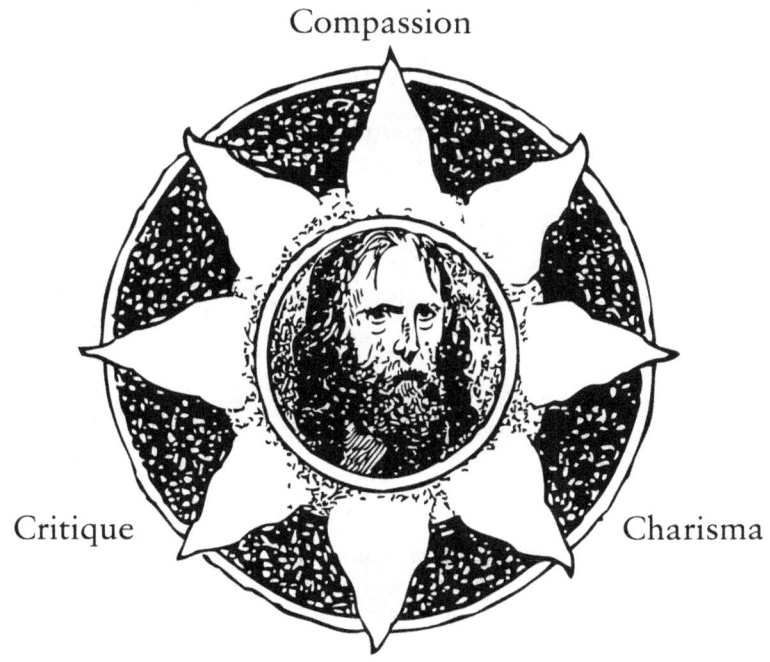

Figure 2: The Liberator's role from multiple perspectives.

§

Hans Kung, who is so well regarded for his work in interfaith dialogue at the Parliament of World Religions, is well placed to assess the role Jesus played. Kung says that if we put Jesus in the cross co-ordinates of the other options in his own tradition or in other religions, and we compare and contrast Jesus in the light of the other options that are presented, then we can see that *Jesus plays the role of a liberator like no one else that we have ever seen in history.* Jesus did not try to play the role of a reformist priest, because he was against the establishment. He did not try to play the part of a traditional rabbi, because he was against legalism. He did not try to play the part of a classical monk, because he was against asceticism. And he did not take up arms and fight as a guerrilla, because he was against violence — from the left as well as the right (see Figure 3).

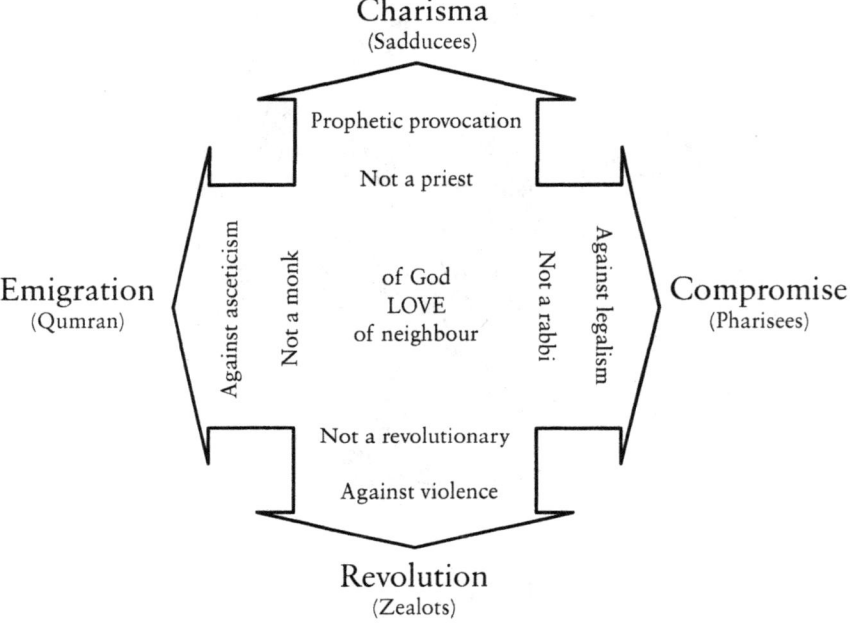

Figure 3: Jesus in the Cross of Co-ordinates of Options within Judaism.[84]

For Jesus, liberation could never come from Saducean rules and regulations, Pharisaic rituals and ceremonies, Qumranic disciplines and practices, or Zealot strategies and tactics. For Jesus, liberation could only ever come through love — real love — substantive, sacrificial, giving and forgiving love — love of God and God's love of our neighbour — love of our friends and love of our enemies.

Jesus did not play the role of a mystic like Buddha, a scholar like Confucius, a lawgiver like Moses, or a military leader like Mohammed. He didn't try to renounce the world and/or study it on the one hand, or try to organize the world and/or control it on the other hand (see Figure 4).

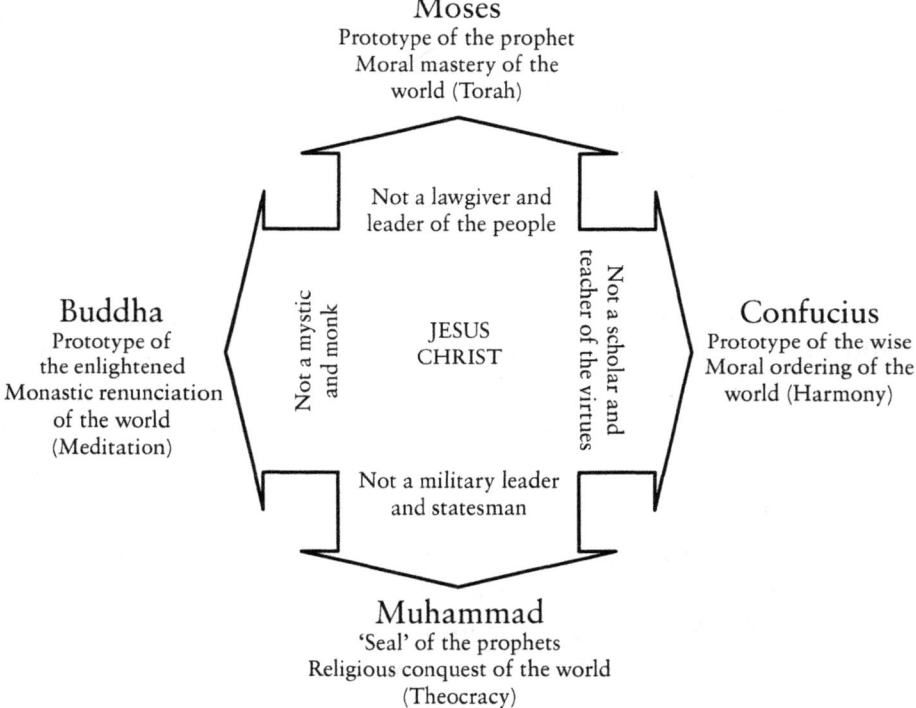

Figure 4: Jesus in the Cross of Co-ordinates of the World Religions.[85]

Jesus loved the world and simply showed people the way that they could love their world like he did. As Baxter Kruger says,

> I am aware of Jesus' astonishing miracles. But [Jesus] spent more time making things with his hands than he performed miracles. He grew up in a family with brothers and sisters and cousins, had a lot of [ordinary] conversations with regular people, celebrated birthdays and went to parties ... [In Jesus] human sharing, human compassion, human love,

> human laughter, human camaraderie and the joy in creativity,
> the pride in design, the delight in making things, were the
> living expression of the humanity of God.[86]

It was never Jesus' intention to start a religion — still less a monopolistic religion that saw itself in competition with other religions for people's allegiance. Jesus said he simply came 'to bring life and life in all its fullness' (see Jn 10:10). Thus he would affirm all that is life-affirming and negate all that is life-negating in the world's religions — especially in the religion that now bears his name...

§

From the moment he was conceived, his mother Mary knew Jesus would be a revolutionary figure: a king who would not only overthrow other kings, but also the very idea of 'kingship' itself; an extraordinary man who would stand, with gentle dignity — against relentless cruelty — for the sake of equality. As far as Mary was concerned, Jesus was the answer to her people's prayers (Lk 1:46–55).

The political economy in which Jesus grew up was one of complete captivity. Palestine was under the complete control of the Roman Empire, abetted by prominent Jewish collaborators. The authorities levied taxes on the population that amounted to forty per cent of people's income. And their taxes were used to maintain the very army of occupation that the people despised. When revolts broke out from time to time, as the people tried to break free of the forces that controlled their lives, the Jewish collaborators aided the Roman colonialists in putting down the rebellions. They cooperated with the very powers that oppressed their own people in order to maintain their position, their property and their monopoly of the market. Not surprisingly, trade and commerce thrived under *Pax Romana*. And the Great Jewish Temple in Jerusalem, combining the roles of Stock Exchange, Central Bank and Government Treasury, became the symbol of that prosperity. However, Israel was still essentially an agrarian society. And agriculture was not only the primary industry, but also the premier industry in society. Thus ownership of land was the main source of wealth Most of the land was owned by a few rich families, who continued to acquire more and more land as the poor families, who couldn't afford to pay their taxes, were forced to sell more and more of their land to pay the taxes that were imposed on them. The poor people, who found themselves without any land at all, found themselves facing a very bleak future indeed. They were forced to confront a cycle of poverty that entailed not only terrible financial insecurity but also total fiscal vulnerability to the very system, which dispossessed them in the first place. In this system the 'poor', the 'prisoners', the 'disabled', 'the disadvantaged', the 'lepers', and other marginalized and disadvantaged people, literally had no place to which they could turn for help. They were helpless.[87]

On one balmy Sabbath, at the very beginning of his ministry, Jesus visited the synagogue in his home town of Nazareth, and when he was asked to read a passage from Holy Scripture, he turned to a part, written by the prophet Isaiah, where it says:

> The Spirit of God has got hold of me,
> And is urging me to take on a special task;
> To share good news with the poor,
> To free the prisoners,
> To help the disabled and the disadvantaged,
> And to smash the shackles of the oppressed... (see Lk 4:18)

In so doing, Jesus announced, in front of everyone he knew at the time, that he wanted to make this radical manifesto his mission in life.

Jesus grew up with a passionate concern for the welfare of his people, particularly those that no one else was particularly concerned for. He was passionately concerned about the plight of the poor, the victims of the imperial system. He was passionately concerned about the predicament of the prisoners, the disabled and disadvantaged, excluded from all meaningful participation in society by bars of steel and stigma. He was passionately concerned about the condition of the lepers, not only because of the pain of their ulcers, but also because of the pain of their untouchability. And he was passionately concerned about the situation of ordinary people whose hope had all but been destroyed by their soul-destroying circumstances, and who consequently felt consigned forever to long days, and even longer nights, of utter despair.

For Jesus, a passionate concern *for* people meant nothing less than a passionate commitment *to* people. He became forgetful of himself, living instead in constant remembrance of those around him who were themselves forgotten. He desperately wanted them to feel fully alive again, to revel in the joy of being loved, and being able to love, once more. He worked tirelessly to set them free from all that might debilitate them, breaking the bonds of exclusivity, poverty, misery, and guilt. He welcomed the outcast, helped the weak, healed the sick, and forgave the sinner, giving them all another chance at a new beginning. He didn't write anyone off himself, and he encouraged everyone that he met not to write one another off either. He challenged everyone to tear up their prejudices, trash their stereotypes, and just get their act together — the 'in' crowd with the outcast; the strong with the weak; the rich with the poor; the saint with the sinner — to support one another in their common quest for their own humanity.

Jesus was painfully aware of the captivity of the political economy in which he lived. He recognized that this captivity was perpetuated by preoccupation with power, position, and property, at the expense of people's lives. 'What the world esteems,' Jesus said, 'is disgusting to God!' (see Lk 16:15). His critique was *universal*, but Jesus actually chose to confront this captivity at a *national* level, rather than an *international* level. Jesus was concerned more with the mechanisms of control perpetuated by his own people, than with the mechanisms of control perpetuated by others. For unless these indigenous mechanisms of control were dealt with, the foreign yoke might be thrown off, but the captivity would continue. So Jesus confronted the people in his own country — the people of his own culture, tradition and religion — with their responsibility for their own captivity, and for their own liberation. 'Don't judge others,' Jesus said. 'Judge yourself' (see Mt 7:1–3). 'How sad it is,' he said to them, that 'you neglect to do justice!'(see Lk 11:42). 'What will it profit them if they gain the whole world but forfeit their life?'(Mt 16:26).

His confrontation of captivity was at a *national* level, but Jesus actually chose to create the alternative communities he advocated at the *local* level, rather than the *national* level. Jesus, the 'Lamb of God' (Jn 1:29), sought to develop his anarchistic communities, of what he called 'flocks of sheep', at the grass roots (see Jn 10:11–16). 'Sheep' was a seemingly innocuous, but essentially subversive term that Jesus used to describe people who lived with 'wolves' — who preyed on other people — but who refused to become wolves themselves. Even if it meant, as Jesus said it might, that the wolves might rip the flock to pieces because of their refusal to join the pack and prey on others. 'I want you to live your lives as sheep, even in the midst of wolves,' said Jesus. 'Be shrewd. But always be harmless' (see Mt 10:16). 'Always treat other people as you would like them to treat you,' he said (see Mt 7:12). 'Even do good to those who do evil to you. Love those who hate you. And bless those who curse you' (see Mt 5:44). 'Do not fear those who kill the body but cannot kill the soul' (Mt 10:28).

In his communities, Jesus encouraged people to liberate themselves from captivity to the political economy, by developing compassion for people that transcended the sick, obsessive, compulsive, preoccupation with power, position, and property that characterised society. 'God is compassionate,' Jesus said. 'Be as compassionate as God' (see Lk 6:35–36).

In these countercultural communities, *Jesus encouraged people to consider other people to be of enormous importance* — not just as producers or consumers, but as people in their own right. The people that were usually considered least important, and consequently pushed to the side, were treated as most important and given a place of respect in these countercultural communities. 'When you throw a party,' Jesus said, 'Do not invite your friends, or your family, or your affluent neighbours. Invite those who have no friends, and those who have no family, and strangers who are anything but affluent' (see Lk 14:12–13).

All oppressive forms of politics were denounced. Charismatic leadership, based on experience, was expected to be exercised within a decision-making framework that functioned according to group consensus. 'We all know the that bosses call the shots, and the heavies throw their weight around,' said Jesus. 'But that is not the way we are going to operate. Whoever wants to be the leader of a group, should be the servant of the group' (see Mt 20:25–26).

All exploitative forms of economics were renounced. Generosity was expected to be exercised, and wealth freely shared by the rich with the poor, in an earnest quest for genuine equality. 'Be on your guard against all kinds of greed,' Jesus said (Lk 12:15); 'Give to everyone who begs from you, and do not refuse anyone who wants to borrow from you' (Mt 5:42); 'lend, expecting nothing in return' (Lk 6:35).

The anarchistic communities Jesus developed never smashed the political economy to which their society was captive. They never completely reconstructed the political economy in terms of the total liberation that they prayed for. However, they did smash some of the mechanisms of control to which they were captive. They managed to reconstruct such a substantial degree of liberated — and liberating — alternative political and economic reality, that their experience has served as an example of true love and true justice ever since. According to eyewitnesses, they all met together, breaking bread in their homes and eating together with glad and jubilant hearts. They had everything in common, selling their possessions and giving support to anyone who asked for help. There wasn't a single person with an unmet need among them, and all the people spoke well of them (see Acts 2:44–47; 4:32–35).

Baxter Kruger comments,

> Jesus Christ was sent to find us and bring us home. And he did just that. He drew us within the circle. He has given us a place in the great dance. This is not something we make true. It is the truth. Jesus is the light of the world. He is the light which illuminates the mystery of our humanity from painting houses and cooking supper to managing a hardware store and friendship, laughter and music. You and your life are the living expression of the glory and joy and beauty and love — the great dance — (of the Trinity).[88]

§

If we look at Rublev's icon carefully, we see the figure in the centre is wearing red — which is a symbol of blood — and so he must have some connection with blood. Also, the red in the cup on the table in front of him is a sign of bloodshed.

It is in the 'bloodshed' — Christ's death on the cross — that the community of God provides us with the *critique*, *charisma* and *catalyst* that is at the crux of the struggle for any movement for genuine personal, social and political change.

A. The Critique of the System

Now the big question is, 'Who killed Christ?' Some might say that God did, going so far as to say, 'God is to blame for everything that goes down in the world.' Some even quote scriptures, such as 'He who did not withhold his own Son, but gave him up for all of us...' (Rom 8:32). Others go so far as to say 'We must understand "delivered up" in its full sense, and not water it down to mean... "give". What happened here [on the cross] is what Abraham did not do to Isaac. (Abraham did not sacrifice Isaac. But God did sacrifice Christ.) He subjected Christ...to death.' You may say to them, 'This is absurd. This wasn't suicide. This was murder. How could God possibly murder God?' No problems, they say. 'In the words of the dogma of the early church: 'The first person of the Trinity annihilates the second.'[89] On the cross Christ is 'godforsaken' — literally 'forsaken by God' — which is why he cries out in a loud voice: *'Eloi, Eloi, lama sabachthani?'* — 'My God, my God, why have you forsaken me?'(Matt 27:46)

But if we read the story of Christ's death on the cross very carefully, it's very clear that God did not kill Christ. Certainly, the Father did 'not withhold his own Son' in the sense that he took the risk to send his Son into the world (Rom 8:32), but when he 'delivered' the Son of God to our doorstep as the Son of Man, he did so saying to himself, 'They will respect my Son' (Mt 21:37). However, when he came, 'his own people did not accept him' (Jn 1:11). He may have been 'the light of the world', but they didn't want him. The people 'loved darkness rather than light because their deeds were evil' and they were afraid that their deeds would be exposed' (Jn 3:19–20). So they decided to get rid of Jesus, and, as he predicted, they eventually seized him and crucified him (see Mt 20:17–19).

To say that Jesus felt 'abandoned by everybody, including God', is quite different from saying that he 'blamed God' for his death. Nailed to that lonely wooden cross, his body wracked with pain, his soul broken with despair, there is no doubt Jesus felt utterly forsaken. And the question arose from deep inside him: 'My God, my God, why have you forsaken me?' But to say Jesus *felt* forsaken, didn't mean that he actually *was* forsaken. In fact, before the agony of crucifixion kicked in, Jesus himself had said, 'Do you think that I cannot appeal to my Father, and he will at once send me more than twelve legions of angels?' (Mt 26:53). And when it was all over, Jesus turned to God, as the only One he felt he could trust, saying, 'Father into your hands I commend my spirit' (Lk 23:46).

It was *not* God who forsook Christ, but his disciples (Mt 26:56b). God was *not* the one who sold him for thirty pieces of silver — it was Judas (Mt 26:14–16). God was *not* the one who denied him three times — it was Peter (Mt 26:69–75). It was *not* God who killed Christ, but the powers that be, aided and abetted by the public (Mt 27:24–26). God was *not* the one who stirred up the crowds — it was the chief priests (Mt 27:1–2, 20–21). God was *not* the one who cried, 'Crucify him! Crucify him!' — it was ordinary people, like you and me (Mt 27:22). And, in the end, it was the authorities — a Jewish King and a Roman Governor — that nailed Christ to the cross (Lk 23:6–25). *Not God!*

'So where was the community of God when all this was happening?' you ask. Well, 'in Christ, God was reconciling the world to himself.' (2 Cor 5:19). God was *in* Christ — in his suffering. God was *in* Christ — in his forsakenness. God was not the perpetrator. God was not a spectator. God was *with the victim*, and God *was the victim*.

Jurgen Moltmann states quite categorically that 'the Father of Jesus is always on Jesus' side — never on the side of the people who crucified him.'[90] He quotes the Scripture, saying: 'Whoever has seen [Jesus] has seen the Father' (Jn 14:9). He goes on to say that 'in the suffering of the Son [is the suffering] of the Father' and poignantly concludes, 'the Father suffers the death of the Son.'[91]

When we read the story of the death of Christ correctly, we are confronted with the most profound and most terrifying critique of humanity in history. For we realize, to our horror, it is not God who has killed Christ, but *the powers that be*, and *people like you and me*, who, in killing Christ, have killed God.

The powers that be are *the authorities* — the spiritual centres of traditions, institutions and systems of control that have immense power over our lives.[92] These cosmic forces — at the heart of our religious traditions, cultural institutions and governmental systems of law and order — maintain their control over our lives through their claims to legitimacy. According to Thomas McAlpine, they claim they have a God-given right to control because as 'properly constituted authorities', they are the 'God-anointed, God-appointed guardians of our lives'.[93] And people like you and me are taught to submit ourselves to the powers that be — whether they are good or bad — so that 'we can learn from God through them'.[94]

However, in his letter to the Colossians, Paul said Jesus 'disarmed the rulers and authorities and made a public example of them' (Col 2:15). In his classic book *Christ and the Powers*, Hendrik Berkhof explains just how Jesus made a public example — or public spectacle — of the 'Powers' on the cross.

> It is precisely in the crucifixion that the true nature of the Powers has come to light. Now that the true God appears on earth in Christ, it becomes apparent that the Powers are inimical to him, not acting as His instruments but as His adversaries. The Scribes, representatives of the Jewish law, far from gratefully receiving Him who came in the name of the God of law, crucified him in the name of the temple. Pilate, representing Roman justice, shows what th[is] is worth when called upon to do justice to the truth Himself. [And] the Pharisees, personifying piety, crucified Him in the name of piety. Obviously 'none of the rulers of this age', who let themselves be worshipped as divinities, understood God's wisdom, 'for if they had known, they would not have crucified the Lord of glory' (1 Cor 2:8). Now they are

unmasked as false gods by their encounter with Very God; they are 'made a public spectacle'.[95]

Walter Wink, in *Engaging the Powers*, writes:

> Jesus died just like all the others who challenge the Powers that dominate the world. [But] some thing went awry [for the Powers] with Jesus. They scourged him with whips, but with each stroke of the lash their own illegitimacy was laid open. They stripped him naked and crucified him in humiliation, all unaware that this very act had stripped them of the last covering that disguised the wrongness of the whole way of living that their violence defended. The law by which he was judged is itself judged, set aside and nailed to the cross. The authorities that publicly shamed him, stripping him naked, have been stripped of their protective covering and exposed as agents of death.[96]

'The very Powers that led [Jesus] to Golgotha are now paraded' as a spectacle for all to see — as they really are!'[97]

However, the Powers are not the only ones seen for 'who they really are' at Golgotha. Peter courageously confronts the people with their complicity, when he stands up publicly in Jerusalem and says, 'Fellow Jews, and all of you who live in Jerusalem (both Jew and Gentile alike), you know Jesus of Nazareth was a man accredited by God, and *you, you* put him to death!'(see Acts 2:14, 22–23). Jesus may have been put to death by *the powers that be*. But, it was only possible because of the collaboration of *people like you and me*.

Gene Sharp, in his seminal study *Power and Struggle*, writes that every Power that there is depends on the support of people for the operationalization of its power. The power that each Power exercises depends on the degree to which people accept its authority, assist with its activities, share their resources with its agencies, and subordinate themselves to its directives. People are prepared to do this for the Powers out of a sense of obligation, a habit of obedience, the desire for approval, the fear of punishment, the hope of reward, or perhaps just plain laziness — taking the path of least resistance.[98]

Jesus acknowledged that people often did not know what they were doing, when they collaborated with the Powers. Even when the crowds, stirred on by the priests, were baying for his blood, he prayed 'Father, forgive them, for they do not know what they are doing' (Lk 23:34). As Studdert Kennedy, the keen observer and remarkable author of *Indifference* writes, 'All through the ages [people] have crucified God, not knowing what they did. Crucified Him through their ignorance, stupidity, dullness of imagination, feebleness of mind, and a host of other factors — as well as their deliberate choice of wrong against right.'[99]

However, at the foot of the cross people are forced to face the truth about themselves at last — clearly, unmistakably, and unavoidably. Here, at the foot of the cross, people are forced to confront the truth of who they are in the light of what they have done. They look at the body in front of them, then look at the blood they have on their hands, and hear that still small voice whispering in their hearts, saying to them: 'You put him to death, you know.' There's no time to run. There's no place to hide. They are totally exposed, and stripped of all excuses. They may have been ignorant, but they know ignorance is no justification. They may have been stupid, but they know stupidity is no defence against culpability. They may not have been too bright — occasionally quite dull, actually — but they know that lack of imagination is hardly an acceptable explanation for the execution of innocents. As feeble and as fickle as people may have been, they know they must own the truth — that out of some misplaced sense of obligation, habit of obedience, desire for approval, fear of punishment, hope of reward, bout of laziness or fit of spite, they have crucified their Messiah, and they have nobody to blame but themselves!

Now, according to the Scripture, although Christ was crucified as an historical event (2 Cor 5:15), he is also crucified 'afresh' (Heb 6:4–6), in an existential sense, every time the powers that be, and people like you and me, conspire to 'crucify' one of our neighbours. Christ makes this very clear when he says that whatever we do to one of the 'least' — the marginalized, distressed, disabled, and disadvantaged —

we do it to him also (see Mt 25:40, 45). He is saying to us: 'When you help them — you help me. And when you hurt them — you hurt me. Whenever you 'crucify' them — I take it personally — it's as if you are actually crucifying me.' 'For the wound of the daughter of my people, is my heart wounded — my grief is beyond healing! (Jer 8:21–22).

When we realize Christ is 'crucified afresh' every time we 'crucify' one of our neighbours, the story of the death of Christ on the cross becomes a metastory we can use to critically reflect, not only on the role the powers that be played in the first century, but also on the role that people like you and me play in the twenty-first century. Thomas Boomershine suggests that a simple way of doing this is to 'identify ways in which the groups with which we are identified are involved in sin [and death]. To meditate on our involvement in the forces that cause abuse, oppression, poverty, and war.' One way you can do that, he says, is to 'identify a communal situation in which you are involved and listen to the story of Jesus' crucifixion in that context.'[100]

When I look for a 'communal situation' that represents the history of the twentieth century, I can't go past the concentration camp. In the early 1900s, the British introduced the idea of the concentration camp as a tool for dealing with the Boers in South Africa. In the middle of the century, the Germans used concentration camps to implement the 'final solution' to the 'Jewish problem'. By the end of the century, the concentration camp was employed in 'killing fields' all over the world — from Cambodia to Kosovo — as the most effective means of pursuing totalitarian policies such as 'cultural revolution and 'ethnic cleansing'. It has become the quintessential symbol of cold-blooded brutality in the bloodiest era on earth — signifying the systematic slaughter of hundreds of millions of innocent men, women and children.

§

The most graphic story I've heard, which connects the concentration camp to the cross, is told by Elie Wiesel in his chilling Nobel prize-winning book *Night*. Wiesel speaks of an execution he witnessed in Auschwitz when he was a 14-year-old boy. Two men and a young boy close to Wiesel's age were suspected of involvement in the sabotage of a power station, and were ordered to be hanged in front of an assembly of prisoners.

> One day when we came back from work, we saw three gallows rearing up in the assembly place, three black crows. Roll call. S.S. all round us, machine guns trained... Three victims in chains — and one of them, the little servant, the sad-eyed angel. The S.S. seemed more preoccupied, more disturbed than usual. To hang a young boy in front of thousands of spectators was no light matter. The head of the camp read the verdict. All eyes were on the child. He was lividly pale, almost calm, biting his lips. The gallows threw its shadow over him. This time the Lagerkapo refused to act as executioner. Three SS replaced him. The three victims mounted together on to the chairs. The three necks were placed at the same moment within the nooses. 'Long live liberty!' cried the two adults. But the child was silent. 'Where is God? Where is He?' someone behind me asked. At a sign from the head of the camp, the three chairs tipped over. Total silence throughout the camp. On the horizon, the sun was setting. 'Bare your heads!' yelled the head of the camp. His voice was raucous. We were weeping. 'Cover your head!' Then the march past began The two adults were no longer alive. Their tongues hung swollen, blue tinged. But the third rope was still moving; being so light, the child was still alive. For more than half an hour he stayed there, struggling between life and death, dying in slow agony under our eyes. And we had to look him full in the face...Behind me, I heard the same man asking: 'Where is God now?' And I heard a voice within me answer him: 'Where is He? Here He is — He is hanging here on this gallows.'[101]

For Elie Wiesel, a deeply religious Jew brought up the Talmud and eager to be initiated into the Cabbala, that evening at sunset became the defining moment of his life.

> Never shall I forget that night, the first night in the camp, which has turned my life into one long night, seven times cursed and seven times sealed. Never shall I forget that stroke. Never shall I forget the little faces of the children whose bodies I saw turned into wreaths of smoke beneath a silent blue sky. Never shall I forget those flames which consumed my faith forever. Never shall I forget that nocturnal silence which deprived me, for all eternity, of the desire to live. Never shall I forget those moments which murdered my God and my soul and turned my dreams to dust. Never shall I forget these things... Never.[102]

Wiesel never did forget. And neither should we. The powers may want us to forget. The people may want us to forget. We may even want to forget ourselves. But we should never forget that the way the world is...is literally killing Christ!

§

In the past few years we have tried to find a way to remind ourselves of this truth in the context in which we live. We've done it by recycling the Stations of the Cross. The Stations of the Cross are traditional series of meditations on the various stages of the story of the cross, from Jesus' trial through to his crucifixion, death and burial. Whereas these meditations used to be more private, we have tried to make them more public. Each Easter a group has gone on an open pilgrimage around our city, seeking to identify — and identify with — the places where Christ is still being 'crucified' in our society.

One place we identified was Brisbane's Planned Parenthood (Abortion) Clinic.

> We may not like to admit it, but we have learned to walk or drive by these specialized killing centres with scarcely a sideways glance or thought as to what goes on behind their doors. We have learned to live with the killing of over 100,000 preborn babies a year [in Australia alone]. [And]

we have learned to accept [even] partial-birth abortions, where six-month old babies are almost completely delivered alive, only to have to be killed by having their brains sucked out by a vacuum machine. Brisbane's Planned Parenthood (Abortion) Clinic is Australia's specialist centre for this particular technique.[103]

Another place we identified was the Tower Mill, on a hill in the middle of Brisbane. The Tower Mill was where the Aborigines who resisted invasion were hanged in the early days of settlement. When the first migrants arrived, there were about 300.000 Aborigines and Islanders in Australia; but after a hundred years of slaughter and resettlement, there were barely 50,000 Aborigines and Islanders left alive.[104] 200 years later, indigenous children still face infant mortality rates three times more than the general population, and a life expectancy of twenty years less than that of any other Australian.[105] And deaths in custody continue to escalate.[106]

Yet another place that, until recently, represented where Christ was being 'crucified' today was the Recruitment Office for the Australian Armed Forces in Brisbane. Since the invasion and occupation of East Timor in 1975 — until sometime in 1999 — the Australian Armed Forces were involved in training of the Indonesian Armed Forces. This included the training of aircraft pilots, combat instructors, military intelligence, and the Special Forces group, Kopassus, who were involved in the wanton massacre of over two hundred thousand people in East Timor.[107] For the Australian Armed Forces to aid the Indonesian Armed Forces in this war against the people of East Timor was particularly reprehensible when you take into account that 40,000 East Timorese gave their lives to help the diggers fighting the Japanese during the Second World War.

The death of God in Christ presents us with a poignant theological critique of systemic injustice, which can spiritually sensitise us to the victims of injustice.

B. The Charisma of Compassion

The Apostle Paul tells us that when Jesus died on the cross, he died *for* our sins (1 Cor 15:3). But what does that word 'for' mean? We know that when Jesus died on the cross, he died 'for' our sins, in the sense that he died *because* of our sins — because we killed him. Yet Paul insists that he not only died 'because of' our sins, but he also died *on behalf of* our sin — for *the sake of* our sins (see 1 Cor 15:3). The question is — what was it that Jesus did on the cross for 'the sake of' our sins?

§

Paul states that 'there is one God, and one mediator between God and human beings, Christ Jesus, himself human, who gave himself as a ransom for all people' (1 Tim 2:5). Furthermore, Peter says that 'you were ransomed from the futile ways you inherited from your ancestors, not with perishable things like silver or gold, but with the precious blood of Christ' (1 Pet 1:18). The word 'ransom' means the price paid for the emancipation or liberation of a person. In the old world it was the price that was paid to free a slave, while in the modern world it is usually the price that is paid to free a hostage. In both cases, the person for whom a ransom has been paid has been 'redeemed' — or 'bought with a price' — phrases that are repeated like a refrain throughout the epistles (1 Cor 6:20; 7:23; Gal 3:13; 4:4).

During the Battle of Adrianople in the fourth century, many prisoners were captured. A message about their plight, with a plea for help, was sent to Ambrose, the Bishop of Milan. Ambrose lived simply, having already given away most of his possessions to help the poor, but he was determined to raise the money needed for a ransom to secure their release. So he took the sacred vessels of the sacrament from off the altar of his church, melted them down, and turned the gold and silver containers into gold and silver coins. He then went and spent all the money he'd collected to ransom the captives. Inevitably there were parishioners who accused Ambrose of acting sacrilegiously. However, the Bishop answered his accusers by saying that the people — for whom Christ's body was broken and Christ's blood was shed — were much more precious than the vessels that carried the symbols of his sacrificial love for them.[108]

The *ransom* story is all about *someone who is prepared to give everything he's got to save someone else*. Which is why the ransom story is such a beautiful picture of what God did for us in Christ.

Offering a 'sacrifice' was a tradition for the Jews that went all the way back to Abraham himself. They had the view that without a sacrifice for sin there could be no salvation. The Jews said that 'without the shedding of blood there is no forgiveness of sins' (Heb 9:22). Messianic Jews, like Peter, saw 'the precious blood of Christ' (1 Pet 1:19) that was poured out on the cross, as the perfect sacrifice for sin:

> He himself bore our sins in his body on the cross, so that, free from sins, we might live for righteousness; by his wounds you have been healed. For you were going astray like sheep, but now you have returned to the shepherd and guardian of your souls. (1 Pet 2:24–25)

This was a poignant allusion to the ancient prophecy of Isaiah:

> But he was sounded for our transgressions,
> crushed for our iniquities;
> upon him was the punishment that made us whole,
> and by his bruises we are healed.
> All we like sheep have gone astray;
> we have turned to our own way,
> and the Lord had laid on him the iniquity of us all.
> (Is 53:5–6)

The metaphor of Christ as someone who was willing to *sacrifice* himself on our behalf can be as powerful a metaphor in the twenty-first century as it was in the first century. There is much about the way the Jews might understand this metaphor that we, as non-Jews, find very difficult to understand. But the idea that someone would be willing to sacrifice his life for us is a very powerful story that touches us deeply.

Telemachus was a monk in the fourth century who sensed that the Spirit was encouraging him to leave his remote Asiatic community and go to Rome, which at that time was like the capital of the world. When Telemachus arrived in the so-called 'heavenly city', Rome was celebrating a recent victory over the troublesome Goths. Telemachus didn't know where he was going, but he allowed the crowds to sweep him along to the Coliseum for the circus that was being held to celebrate the victory. What he saw there horrified him. There was gut-wrenching carnage, as gladiators fought one another to the death to entertain the bloodthirsty crowds.

Telemachus felt that he had to do something. He simply couldn't stand by idly and do nothing while human beings were being beheaded, disemboweled and dismembered before his very eyes. So he ran down the steps of the stands, leapt into the arena and began darting between the fighters, crying, 'Forbear. Forbear. In the name of Christ I beg you to forbear.'

When the crowd saw the scrawny figure of the monk running frantically about the arena, ducking and weaving between the combatants, they took Telemachus to be a bit of comic relief, and roared their approval. However, some of the people in the crowd began to hear what 'the mad monk' was saying, and as they came to realize that Telemachus was actually trying to spoil their bloody fun, they turned against him, hissing, booing and bellowing at the top of their voices for his quick dispatch.

What happened next no one seems to know for sure. We do know that the gladiators lunged at the monk and that the audience buried him under a hailstorm of stones. When the furore was over, Telemachus lay dead in the middle of the arena.

Then a strange thing happened. In the silence that ensued, it was as if the monk's last cry echoed eerily around the arena once again: 'Forbear. Forbear. In the name of Christ, I beg you to forbear.' Overcome with shame, the spectators departed, leaving the circus empty, never to return. Never again did an audience gather to watch people butcher each other at the Coliseum in Rome. All brutal gladiatorial battles were banned. And Telemachus was written into the pages of history as the hero who, single-handedly, brought the era of slaughter as entertainment to an end.[109]

It is likely that the declining power of the empire, resulting in diminishing numbers of recruits for gladiatorial schools and decreasing amounts of funds available to stage gladiatorial contests, were also very significant factors in putting an end to the circus. However, Telemachus will always be remembered as the man who, in the end, was actually prepared to *sacrifice* his life to save people in the arena from slaughter.[110]

The sacrifice story is all about *someone who is prepared to lay down their own life to save the lives of others*. Which is why sacrifice is such a magnificent picture of what God did for us in Christ.

§

On the cross God proved to us, once and for all, beyond any shadow of a doubt, that he is the kind of person who is always prepared to give everything he's got to help someone else. *This is the gospel. This is the good news*. That God is indeed good. So good, in fact, that he is far better than we could have ever imagined that he might be. He is actually willing to give everything he's got in order to help us — even to the extent of being willing to lay down his own life for us. Jesus' life and death is God's guarantee of our liberation.

But the question remains: Why the necessity of this *sacrifice* for the forgiveness of sins? Why the necessity of having to pay such a heavy price, in blood, to *ransom* our souls? There is no biblical evidence to suggest that the ransom was the price paid to the Devil. And there is no biblical evidence to suggest that the sacrifice was offered to God to give him his 'pound of flesh' before he was willing to forgive us. Quite to the contrary. Scripture says God is always more than willing to forgive and being willing to forgive means being willing to relinquish any right to retaliation — the opposite of demanding any kind of vindictive satisfaction. So why, we may well ask, the need for Christ to be 'the atoning sacrifice for our sins?' (1 Jn 1:1–2; Jn 3:16–17; 1 Jn 2:2).

My view is that there never was, and never will be, any forgiveness without *sacrifice*. Forgiveness, by definition, means making the sacrifice that is necessary to accept an injustice without demanding satisfaction in return. The greatness of any single act of forgiveness consists in the greatness of the sacrifice that a person is prepared to make in relinquishing their right to restitution or retaliation in order to restore a relationship. The greatness of forgiveness is in exact proportion to the greatness of the sacrifice. It is my view that throughout the ages God had always been prepared to suffer greatly to forgive greatly. However, because God was invisible, no one saw the tears that God cried. Only the prophets, who lived in sympathy with the heart of God, had any appreciation of the greatness of his *grace*. Until, at the right time, God stepped onto the stage of human history, visibly, as a human being, and, in Jesus, showed us just how great his grace is. God's grace is great enough to embrace our pain, absorb our rage, forgive our sin, and encourage us all towards completely revolutionary personal growth and social change. *In Jesus on the cross, we can see that God embraces our pain.*

Frederick Beuchner tells a story that he says is 'a peculiarly twentieth-century story'. You only have to hear the story once to know that it's just the kind of story that Jesus himself might have told.

> It's a kind of parable of the lives of all of us. It's about a boy of twelve or thirteen who, in a fit of crazy anger got hold of a gun and fired it at his father, who did not die straight away but soon afterward. When [he] was asked why he had done it, he said that he could not stand his father, because his father demanded too much of him. And then later on, after he had been placed in a house of detention, a guard was walking down the corridor late one night when he heard sounds from the boy's room, and he stopped to listen. The words that he heard the boy sobbing out in the dark were, 'I want my father, I want my father.'

'Our father,' Beuchner says, 'we have killed him, and we will kill him again.'[III] However, Jesus, on the cross, cries out as one of us, saying 'Father, Forgive them; for they do not know what they are doing'(Lk 23:34).

In Jesus on the cross, we see God not only embraces our pain, he also absorbs our rage. Gale Webbe, in *The Night and Nothing*, writes,

> There are many ways to deal with evil. All of them are facets of the truth that the only ultimate way to conquer evil is to let it be smothered within a willing, living, human being. When it is absorbed there, like a spear into one's heart, it loses its power and goes no further.[112]

As M Scott Peck writes in *The People Of The Lie*, 'The healing of evil can only be accomplished by love. A willing sacrifice is required. The healer must sacrificially absorb the evil.'[113] Jesus on the cross absorbed our evil; he took it into his heart as assuredly as the spear that was thrust into his side. And, it went no further; there was no reaction, no demand for restitution, no demand for retaliation. The cycle of violence stopped right there and then, with him, forever.

In Jesus on the cross, we see God not only absorbs our rage, he also forgives our sin. 'One thing I know,' William Barclay says,

> that because of Jesus Christ and what he did [on the cross] my relationship to God is changed. Prior to Jesus Christ [we] did not fully know what God was like. The holiness of God [we] did know; but the marvel of the love of God [we] had never dreamed of. When Jesus healed the sick, comforted the sad, fed the hungry and forgave his enemies, he was saying, 'God loves you like that. Nothing that [you] can ever do will stop God loving [you].' Because of Jesus Christ I know God is my friend. He is no longer my enemy. He is no longer even my judge. There is no longer any unbridgeable gulf between him and me. Daily, and hourly, I experience the fact that I can enter into his presence with confidence. [And as a result] I am more at home with God than I am with any other human being in the human world.[114]

Last, but not least, *in Jesus on the cross we see God not only forgives our sin, he also encourages us all towards completely revolutionary personal growth and social change.* When I gaze at Jesus on the cross my heart is strangely moved. Someone dying for a cause doesn't make it right. But a manifesto of love written in blood cannot easily be dismissed. A movement, which has proved to be worth dying for, may lay claim to be worth living for. The martyrdom of Jesus lights a beacon for compassion — an inextinguishable fire that scorches the apathy and hypocrisy hidden in the dark corners of my soul. His agony breaks my heart, and, in the process, breaks down some of my barriers I have erected in my heart against my own humanity. His anguish brings the sound of others crying to my ears which otherwise I would not hear, and brings the sight of others suffering to my eyes which otherwise I would not see. For me, the death of Jesus is not the end, but the beginning — of a whole new way of life committed to the way of Jesus.

The death of Christ demonstrates the fact that God's grace is great enough to embrace our pain, absorb our rage, forgive our sin, and to encourage us all towards completely revolutionary personal growth and social change.

C. The Catalyst For Transformation

One of the problems people have with Christians is that we are not only un-Christ-like, but we also use our Christian theology to rationalize our continuing to be un-Christ-like. After all — as the bumper stickers emblazoned on our cars boldly proclaim — we're 'Not perfect — Just forgiven!' Mahatma Gandhi was not afraid to confront Christians with our misuse of the theology of the cross in rationalizing our continued un-Christ-likeness. In his famous autobiography *Experiments With Truth*, Gandhi describes an encounter he had with an evangelical Christian:

> Mr Coates was a staunch young man...he introduced me to several friends whom he regarded as staunch Christians. One of these introductions was to a family that belonged to the Plymouth Brethren...During my contact with this family, the Plymouth Brethren confronted me with an argument for which I was not prepared: 'You cannot understand the beauty of our religion. You must be brooding over your transgressions every moment of your life, always mending them and atoning for them. How can this ceaseless cycle

of action bring you redemption? You can never have peace.
Now look at the perfection of our belief. You admit we
are all sinners. Our attempts at improvement are futile. Yet
redemption we must have. How can we bear the burden of
sin? We can but throw it on Jesus. He is the only sinless Son
of God. It is his word that those who believe in him shall
have everlasting life. As we believe in the atonement of Jesus,
our own sins do not bind us. Sin we must. It is impossible to
live in this world sinless. Therefore Jesus atoned for all the
sins of mankind. Only he who accepts his great redemption
can have eternal peace. Think what a life of restlessness is
yours — what a promise of peace we have.'[115]

Many Christians would have thought this was a pretty convincing presentation of the gospel, but Gandhi says that 'the argument failed to convince me'. And the reason that this presentation of the gospel failed to convince Gandhi is worth considering. Gandhi says,

> I humbly replied: If this be Christianity acknowledged by all
> Christians, I cannot accept it. [For] I do not seek redemption
> from the consequences of my sin. I seek to be redeemed
> from sin itself — [even] the very thought of sin. Until I have
> attained that, I shall be content to be restless.[116]

Gandhi did not question the theology of the cross that he was presented with because he wanted to 'continue in unrighteousness'. Quite the contrary. Gandhi said that he desired to be righteous with all his heart — to be redeemed from sin — not merely the consequences of sin. He questioned the theology of the cross he was presented with because he felt that it was being used as a rationalization for continuing in sin. 'Sin we must,' it went. 'It is impossible to live in this world sinless.' Only Jesus 'is sinless'.

Now I think that it is quite interesting to note that a number of the apostles had similar concerns to the Mahatma. Paul asked the question: 'Shall we sin because we are not under law but under grace?' His own resolute answer to the question comes down to us through the centuries, as clearly as ever, crying, 'Never! Your body should be an instrument of righteousness' (see Rom 6:15–23). John writes, 'If we confess our sins, he who is faithful and just will forgive us our sins, and cleanse us from all unrighteousness' — not only from the consequences of unrighteousness, but also from what he calls 'all unrighteousness' itself (1 Jn 1:7–9).

§

Jesus taught his disciples to pray for God's will to 'be done on earth as it is in heaven' (Mt 6:10).[117] Whenever they failed to do this, he taught them ask for forgiveness. That forgiveness was unmerited, because all forgiveness, by definition, is unmerited. However, the forgiveness he taught them to ask for was conditional, not unconditional. He taught them to say, 'Forgive us our debts, as we also have forgiven our debtors' (Mt 6:12), and he lets his disciples know that he means what he says. He tells them, 'For if you forgive others their trespasses, your heavenly Father will also forgive you; but if you do not forgive others, neither will your Father forgive your trespasses' (Mt 6:14–15). The point is obvious, and Christ repeats it in order to drive the point home. Grace can never, ever, be earned, but it is given to us on the condition that we give it to others.

When the disciples asked how often they were required to forgive someone, Jesus said, 'If another disciple sins, you must rebuke the offender, and if there is repentance, you must forgive. And if the same person sins against you seven times a day, and turns back to you seven times and says, "I repent", you must forgive' (Lk 17:3–4). On another occasion he said to the disciples, 'Actually, make that not seven times, but seventy-seven times!' (see Mt 18:21–22). Again, the point is obvious. Because we have experienced grace we should extend grace — in this case, by extending forgiveness to others. And if others are to experience grace, they are to extend grace — in this case, by extending an apology to us. So it goes on — seventy times seven — or *ad infinitum* — until the whole world is full of the grace of God.

Jesus stressed the importance of this process to his disciples by telling them a parable. He said that the Kingdom of Heaven on Earth is like a king who decided to settle accounts with his servants (Mt 18:23–34). One servant owed him millions of dollars, but the master took pity on him, cancelled his debt, and set him free.

> But that same slave, as he went out, came upon one of his fellow-slaves who owed him a hundred denarii; and seizing him by the throat, he said, 'Pay what you owe.' Then his fellow-slave fell down and pleaded with him, 'Have patience with me, and I will pay you.' But he refused; then he went and threw him into prison until he should pay the debt. When his fellow-slaves saw what had happened, they were greatly distressed, and they went and reported to their lord all that had taken place. Then his lord summoned him and said to him, 'You wicked slave! I forgave you all that debt because you pleaded with me. Should you not have had mercy on your fellow-slaves, as I had mercy on you?' And in anger his lord handed him over to be tortured until he should pay his entire debt. (Mt 18:28–34)

When he had finished the story, Jesus turned to his disciples and pointedly said, 'So my heavenly Father will also do to every one of you, if you do not forgive your brother or sister from your heart' (Mt 18:35). Note that the same man who said, 'Father, forgive them, for they know not what they do,' is saying, 'unless you forgive your brother or your sister from your heart, your heavenly Father will not forgive you.' He is saying that forgiveness is offered freely to all, but it can only be ours if we give it to others in the same way that it has been given to us.

Just to be sure we've got the message correctly, let's just stay with the story a while and unpack the narrative, piece by piece, as a parable of the process of salvation. Was the servant who owed his master an unpayable debt doomed when it came to settling his account with the master? Yes. When the master decided to cancel his debt, was he saved? Yes. Was this salvation unmerited? Yes. Was this salvation unconditional? No. So what was the unwritten, but understood, condition of that salvation? That the servant would extend the same grace extended to him to his fellow servants.

The moral of the story is that 'salvation' — or what these days we would call 'liberation' — is about unmerited, but not unconditional, grace. It's about the cycle of alternately receiving and sharing God's grace 'from your heart'.

§

If we understand anything at all about grace, we will not want to say or do anything that puts the salvation of others at risk, but we may be willing to put our own salvation at risk in order to save others. After all, the gospel is all about participating whole-heartedly in the experience of extending God's amazing, but very risky grace, to the whole world.

The protagonists of salvation in both testaments in the Bible show they understood this very well. For example, take Moses, the 'greatest prophet' in the Old Testament, and Paul, the 'greatest apostle' in the New Testament. Both Moses and Paul at times were actually prepared to put their own salvation at risk in order to try to save other people.

Moses came down from Mount Sinai, having received the Ten Commandments, only to find the people in open revolt, dancing round the idol of a golden calf. God was furious and threatened the people with punishment. Moses knew that God was furious — after all, he was furious with the people himself. However, to save the people from destruction, Moses offered to try to intervene with God on their behalf. 'So Moses returned to the Lord and said, "Alas, this people has sinned a great sin; they have made for themselves gods of gold. But now, if only you will forgive their sin — but if not, blot me out of the book [of life] that you have written".' (Ex 32:31–32). God told Moses that there was no way he would punish the innocent on behalf of the guilty. However, *Moses was prepared to sacrifice his salvation to save others.*

Paul, as a Jew, struggled with the implications of his people's rejection of Jesus as their Christ.

> I am speaking the truth in Christ — I am not lying; my conscience confirms it by the Holy Spirit — I have great sorrow and unceasing anguish in my heart. For I could wish that I myself were accursed and cut off from Christ for the sake of my own people, my kindred according to the flesh. (Rom 9:1–3)

It seems that Paul valued salvation so much that he couldn't stand by, holding on to his salvation, while the people he loved, lost it. *He said he was 'not lying' when he said that he was more than willing to sacrifice his salvation to save others.*

In their willingness to sacrifice their safety and their security — even their salvation — in order to save others, Moses and Paul both point to the perfect sacrificial attitude that Jesus Christ displayed on the cross.

> Those who passed by derided him, shaking their heads and saying, 'You who would destroy the temple and build it in three days, save yourself! If you are the Son of God, come down from the cross.' In the same way the chief priests also, along with the scribes and elders, were mocking him, saying, 'He saved others; he cannot save himself. He is the King of Israel; let him come down from the cross now, and we will believe in him.' (Mt 27:39–42)

However, he did not come down from the cross, and as a result many people lost faith in him. Yet whether they believed him or not, Christ was willing to endure the cross. Not because he *could* not save himself, but because he *would* not save himself. He was more concerned about saving the people ridiculing him than he was about saving himself. *He did not come 'to be served, but to serve, and to give his life a ransom for many'* (Mt 20:28).

When Jesus was asked about his willingness to sacrifice his life for others, he simply replied that he was the Good Shepherd, who lays down his life for his sheep (Jn 10:11–15). For Jesus, it seems, the matter of sacrifice was as straightforward as that.

§

At the Last Supper, the final meal Jesus had with his disciples before his execution, Jesus told the disciples about his understanding of the meaning of his crucifixion. He took the bread, broke it into pieces, and said, 'Take, eat; this is my body.' Then he took the wine, poured it out for them, and said, 'Drink from it, all of you; for this is my blood of the [new] covenant, which is poured out for many for the forgiveness of sins' (Mt 26:26–28).

A covenant is a special relationship people commit themselves to. The *old covenant* was a special relationship that God entered into with the people of Israel (Ex 24:1–8). It was a reciprocal agreement based on God's commitment to care for the people, and the people's commitment to cooperate with God. The terms of the agreement were outlined in the law (Ex 24:7). If the people broke the law there was a provision for reconciliation based on the offering of a blood sacrifice with a penitent heart. The sacrifice was not required to appease the anger of God, but to remind the sinner of the awfulness of their sin in breaking their agreement. However, these sacrifices proved to have real limitations in effecting real changes in people's hearts — The blood of goats sprinkled on those who were ceremonially unclean, made them outwardly, but not inwardly, 'clean' (see Heb 9:13).

The *new covenant* was different from the old covenant in two important respects. Firstly, it was recognized as being a relationship that was based on love rather than on law. Secondly, it was a relationship that was restored, not by any sacrifice we might make to God, but by the sacrifice that God, in Christ, made for us. Of course, the hope was that the new covenant, written on our hearts in the 'blood of Christ', would 'purify our conscience from dead works to worship the living God!' (Heb 9:14). For Paul, the new covenant was the good news, and he encouraged us to celebrate the good news of this new covenant regularly at the Lord's Supper. 'Do this,' the Lord says, 'whenever you eat this bread and drink this cup' in 'remembrance of me' (see 1 Cor 11:23–27).

Now, one of the crucial questions that face us, is 'What does this mean for us?' What does it mean for us to 'do this in remembrance of

Jesus' today? Carlos Christos, a Catholic from a middle-class family in Brazil — who got involved as a lay brother working with the poor, and was put into prison for four years for his efforts — spent a period of time in prison trying to answer this question. In a letter from prison to his parents he wrote:

> He took into his hands those most ordinary of foods, bread and wine, and he consecrated them. 'This is my body which will be broken for you. This is my blood which will be shed for you. Do this in memory of me.' What is the meaning of these words we repeat every Mass? When the priest repeats the words in the Mass, 'Do this in memory of me,' I interpret it as Jesus saying to us: 'I have loved you completely, so much that I willingly died for you. I've given all that I am to free you. Having nothing left but my life, I didn't grudge you that either. I gave it up to show you that the limits of love are to love without limits. I have given you my body and my blood. I have made this gesture a sacrament so that at any time or place in human history you may receive it and re-enact it in your own life. When I said, 'Do this in memory of me,' I did not mean you should merely commemorate what I had done. I meant you should do likewise, that you should offer your body and blood for the redemption of humanity. Just as at the Mass you receive my body and blood, so in your lives you should offer up your own, so that my acts may always be present in the world through you.' (The) Mass is something to be lived rather than attended, and that it is to be lived to the extent that we are willing to sacrifice ourselves for the liberation of human beings, and so become God's sacrament in the world.[118]

§

Carlos Christos is correct. We are called not only to receive the sacrifice of Christ, but also to re-enact the sacrifice of Christ, by repeating his redemptive acts in our own life. Jesus instituted his new covenant with a new commandment. The old commandment had been that 'you shall love your neighbour as yourself' (Lev 19:18). However, Jesus said, 'I give you a new commandment, that you love one another. Just as I have loved you, you also should love one another' (Jn 13:34). Now the big difference that there is between the old commandment and the new commandment is simply the way in which we are called to love one another. In the *old* covenant we are expected to love our neighbour as we have loved ourselves, but in the *new* covenant we are expected to love our neighbour as Christ has loved us. It is loving one another *as Christ has loved us*, that is the quintessential characteristic of the *new covenant* that Christ inaugurated on the cross.

Note that the new commandment is about loving, not about suffering. We are called to love, not to suffer. But, if suffering is necessary to do justice in the face of injustice, then so be it. The call to love, in that case, is a call for us to suffer for others in the same way as Christ suffered for us.

> It is to your credit if, being aware of God, you endure pain while suffering unjustly. If you endure when you are beaten for doing wrong, where is the credit in that? But if you endure when you do right and suffer for it, you have God's approval. For to this you have been called, because Christ also suffered for you, leaving you an example, so that you should follow in his steps. (1 Pet 2:19–21)

The telling word in that sentence is the word Peter used in his letter for 'example'. It is *hupogrammos*, which designates the perfect line of writing at the top of an exercise book, that anyone who wants to learn to write, needs to learn to copy as closely as they can. So Peter is saying that 'we need to copy Christ as closely as we can when it comes to developing our capacity to suffer for the sake of love'.[119] In his Epistle to the Philippians, Paul unpacks the implications of Christ's example for us:

> Each of you should not look to your own interests, but also to the interests of others. You should have exactly the same

attitude as Christ Jesus had: For he who had always been God by nature, did not cling to his prerogatives as God's equal; instead, he stripped himself of all privilege, emptied himself, and made himself nothing, in order to be born by nature as a mortal. And, having become a human being, he humbled himself, living the life of a slave, a life of utter obedience, even unto death. And the death he died, on the cross, was the death of a common criminal. (see Phil 2:4–8)

This is an extraordinary exhortation to a degree of self-forgetful sacrificial love that staggers the imagination of most ordinary mortals. Yet Paul seems to expect that people like you and me can incarnate exactly the same attitude as Christ Jesus had. He expects us to empty ourselves of our own preoccupations and make more time and space for others. He expects us empathize with others and join them in their struggle to love and be loved. And he expects us empower others and support them in their quest to live their lives to the full — even if it kills us.

3. THE SUSTAINER

The haloes suggest that community
won't work without a spirituality
Not just any spirituality — a healthy,
holistic, holy spirituality of love.
The colour green is a symbol of energy, growth,
new life. The figure on the right is wearing green
and is associated with growth and new life

Reading Rublev's icon from left to right, the third person from the left is the third person in the Trinity — the One we'll call the 'Sustainer'.

In the person of Christ, the Liberator is God 'incarnate' — the recognisable human face of God. However, in the Spirit, the Sustainer is God *'incognito'* — the self-effacing face of God — who has no face but our face to demonstrate grace. The Liberator comes alongside us, as one of us, and models love for us, but the Sustainer is inside us, inspiring us with amazing love for others ourselves.

Through the Spirit, God energises us. In fact our English word 'enthusiasm' comes from the Greek *en-theos* or 'in-god'. This suggests that if we want to maintain our enthusiasm, then we need to be filled with the Spirit. The Spirit enhances our *vitality*, *sensitivity* and *responsibility*, so that we have the power to struggle for real personal, social and political change (see Figure 5).

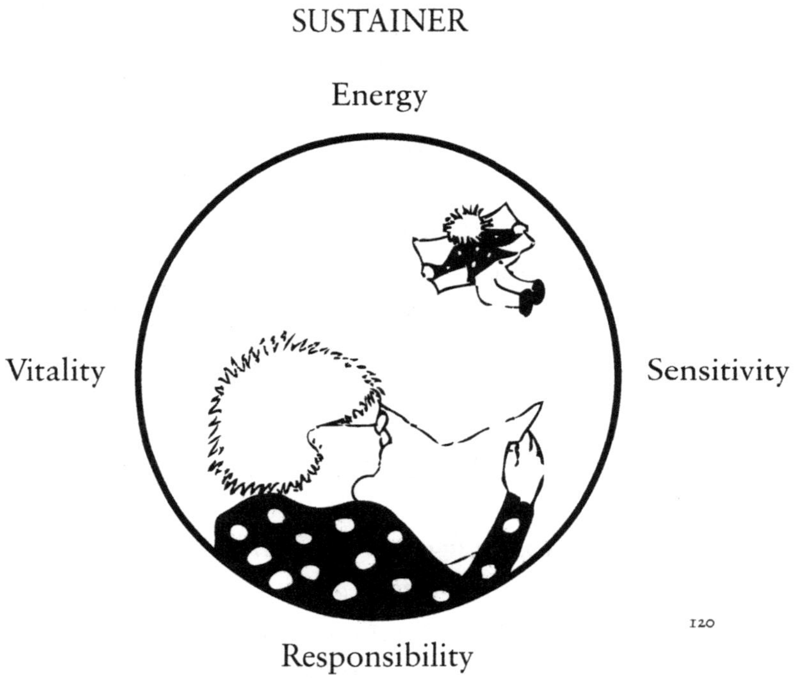

SUSTAINER

Energy

Vitality   Sensitivity

Responsibility

120

Figure 5: The role of the Sustainer in our struggle for genuine personal, social and political change.

A. The Source Of Vitality and Sensitivity

Traditionally referred to as the 'Holy Spirit' or simply the 'Spirit', the Sustainer takes great delight in breathing vitality into our troubled souls. The words used in the Bible for 'spirit' are the Hebrew *ruach* and the Greek *pneuma*. Both these words refer to moving air like wind and/or breath that you can't actually see, but the effects of which are visible. This conveys the idea that the role of the Sustainer is vital, but essentially anonymous, as easily overlooked as the significance of the next breath we take — until we find that we can't take it for granted anymore.

Ann Armstrong recently wrote an article for the *Guardian* newspaper in which she spoke about her experience, as a polio sufferer, of being on a mechanical respirator that had helped her to breathe artificially for the last twenty years:

> …with the puff from my mechanical respirator I cannot make a such a powerful shout [as I did with] my own lungs which helped me to introduce myself to the world with my first yell. In consequence I am always softly spoken and those around me can have no idea of the intensity of my passion — or the commotion I would like to make at times.[121]

None of us who breathes without a mechanical respirator can truly appreciate Ann's experience. However, all of us know what it's like to be winded or breathless, and how completely debilitating that can be — if only for a few minutes. We desperately feel the need to take a deep breath in order to function.[122] This is precisely the role of what the fifteenth-century mystic poet, Kabir, called 'the breath inside the breath'— to help us to function fully as human beings.[123]

While images of 'wind' and 'breath' seem impersonal, the impact of the Spirit always stirs within us the deepest sense of ourselves as persons. Ann says that in only being able to take a shallow puff, she doesn't have the energy to express herself the way she would like to — the way she really is, but which nobody really knows. She says that she could only express the great passion she feels deep down if she were able to take a really deep breath. Aubrey Johnson suggests that, according to the Jewish Bible, it is only as we take a really deep breath and are filled with the Spirit that we can fully express the whole range of our emotional, intellectual, and volitional life.[124]

This point is clearly illustrated in the Old Testament narrative of the prophet Ezekiel's vision of The Valley of Dry Bones (Ez 37). Paul

Fiddes comments that,

> ...in his vision of the valley of dry bones the prophet Ezekiel is addressing a nation at the depths of depression. They feel like just like a heap of dried-up bones lying on the open ground, bleaching white in the heat of the midday sun. And then Yahweh speaks his promise; he will come like the wind (like a breath of fresh air), he will give them life so that they will stand on their feet once more, not as a heap of broken human wreckage, but a great army, ready for action.

According to Fiddes,

> ...this is not a picture of resurrection of the individual beyond death, but the revival of a whole nation within history...God will breathe within it; and the four winds of the earth will blow, raising it up as dried leaves are whirled up from the ground by the force of a gale...[Thus] the coming of the spirit here is like breath within and breath beyond, stirring deep and taking people into its flow.[125]

§

Jesus said there is always a mystery about the way the Spirit breathes vitality into our lives. Sometimes it comes screaming into our lives like a gale-force storm, rattling through the valley of dry bones at the bottom of our souls. But probably, most times, it comes with a whisper on a zephyr of wind that gusts so gently that we scarcely notice it speaking a 'still small word' into our subconscious minds. Jesus said no one really knows how or when or where it will come. He said 'the wind blows where it chooses, and you hear the sound of it, but you do not know where it comes from or where it goes' (Jn 3:8). However, Jesus said that the one thing that is necessary, is to be open to it when it does come — so we can make the most of the opportunity we have to be 'born [again] of the Spirit' (Jn 3:8).

Jesus told his disciples about the role of the Spirit in his life. He said it was not duty, or obligation, or rules and regulations, but the Spirit that was at the heart of being who he was and doing what he was doing (see Lk 4:18). He set the disciples an example, shared with them some principles that were important to him, and encouraged them to experiment with some of his core practices themselves. However, he said that unless they were energized by the Spirit, there was just no way that they would be able to sustain a life of radical non-violent sacrificial compassion. He tried to pass on the Spirit to them (Jn 20:22), but for some reason or other, they didn't get it. So the last thing he told them, before he left, was not to go anywhere until they were 'filled with the Spirit'. He said that sooner or later, the day would come when they would all be 'immersed' in the Spirit, and if they were empty, open, receptive and created a hospitable space in their hearts, then when they were 'immersed' in the Spirit, they would naturally be filled with the 'Spirit' as well (see Acts 1:4–5).

So in order to create a hospitable space in their hearts for the Spirit, once Jesus left, the disciples spent time together constantly in prayer (Acts 1:14). For the disciples, prayer was a process of developing an awareness of, and availability to, the Spirit. It involved waiting upon the Spirit and a willingness to yield to the Spirit. It was essentially a desire to live life wholly and solely in the *joie de vivre* of the Spirit. Prayer had an important place in their life together, because they recognised that the *joie de vivre* of the Spirit was the centre of energy that they needed for community and community development. Prayer became the still point around which the life of the community revolved, the point of integration where the conflicts in the community were resolved, the starting point at which people began to live again, and the point of departure from which people began to experiment with another way of living (Acts 1:12–26).

The disciples prayed *constantly* because they had come to realise that true community did not begin and end with them, but with the Spirit; it was in prayer that they could encounter the Spirit who is the beginning and the end of the community development process. They realised that it was only in encounter with the Spirit that all that was good could be affirmed, all that was evil could be confronted, and their task for the future outlined. A vision of justice could be revealed, an infusion of grace could be realized, and they could access the vitality they needed to practise the sensitivity required to engage in the struggle for the 'salvation' of the world.

§

When the Spirit came at Pentecost, the disciples were ready for it. Even then, it was a completely unexpected, surprisingly wild and wonderful ride…

> When the day of Pentecost had come, they were all together in one place. And suddenly from heaven there came a sound like the rush of a violent wind, and it filled the entire house where they were sitting. Divided tongues, as of fire, appeared among them, and a tongue rested on each of them. All of them were filled with the Holy Spirit and began to speak in other languages, as the Spirit gave them ability.
> Now there were devout Jews from every nation under heaven living in Jerusalem. And at this sound the crowd gathered and was bewildered, because each one heard them speaking in the native language of each…All were amazed and perplexed, saying to one another, 'What does this mean?' But others sneered and said, 'They are filled with new wine.' But Peter, standing with the eleven, raised his voice and addressed them: 'Men of Judea and all who live in Jerusalem, let this be known to you, and listen to what I say. Indeed, these are not drunk, as you suppose, for it is only nine o'clock in the morning. No, this is what was spoken through the prophet Joel:
> "In the last days it will be, God declares, that I will pour out my Spirit upon all flesh."' (Acts 2.1–6; 12–18)

I think that we can identify with both kinds of reactions to this event. We might start out saying to ourselves 'These people are out of their minds,' but probably end up asking ourselves the big question: 'What does all this mean?' Well, I think this event means many things.

§

The role of the Spirit may be dramatic at times, but is always anonymous. We hear the wind, look around to see who is there, and, on an occasion such as this see 'tongues of fire', but on most other occasions probably see nothing at all. Even when there are tongues of fire, they act as signs that point to the people, singling out otherwise singularly unimportant anonymous people — most of whose names we do not know and never do get to know — as the centre of attention on this particular occasion.

The apostle Paul says that this is typical of the self-effacing way the Spirit works. In writing to the faith community at Corinth, he says,

> Consider your own call, brothers and sisters: not many of
> you were wise by human standards, not many were powerful,
> not many were of noble birth. But God chose what is foolish
> in the world to shame the wise; God chose what is weak
> in the world to shame the strong. God chose what is low
> and despised in the world, things that are not, to reduce to
> nothing things that are...(1 Cor 1:26–28)

Peter says that now ordinary people need no longer be subject to the prophets, priests and kings who traditionally ruled their lives, because — through the power of the Spirit — they have become 'a chosen race, a royal priesthood, a holy nation' (1 Pet 2:9). And now, as prophetic people, they can bear witness to God's agenda of love and justice for the world; as priestly people, they can intercede for those in need themselves; and as royal people, they can actually anticipate and represent the kingdom of heaven on earth.[126]

The 'tongues of fire' are a symbol of the way the Spirit takes 'nobodies', like these poor despised uneducated Galileans and — to the surprise of everybody — makes them 'somebodies.' As we know, fire has always been an archetypal image of passion. It's common for us to say that someone 'burns with desire'. When the Spirit comes at Pentecost, it puts people in touch with their passion. The Spirit does not put people in touch with an abstract ideal or heroic image of themselves, but with the reality of their true selves — stirring their desire to be the person that deep down they really want to be. Relating to each one individually, the Spirit fills the hospitable space they have created in their hearts with a burning desire to become the person that God has created them to be.

Baxter Kruger writes,

> The New Testament refers to the Spirit as the 'Spirit of truth' and as the 'Spirit of adoption'...we don't hear much about adoption, the staggering reality of our inclusion in [the community of God]...the virtual silence on our adoption leave us in the dark about our true identity.[127]

> ...To believe that we are not included means we believe we are outside the circle, excluded from glory and meaning, excluded from life — both in the sense of life as existence itself and in the sense of life as animation...[The Spirit] is the one who gives us a reason to believe that we are included in God's circle, included in the 'glory and meaning' of God's life, included in God's 'passion and joy. The Spirit is the 'life of the party'. In and through [the Spirit] the great dance is shared with us. Sharing of the dance always bears witness with our spirits that we are not our own, but belong to God... because of the Spirit we know who we are and we are restless until the life we live matches the life we know is ours.[128]

Paul talks about the powers of the Spirit as the energies for a new life (see 1 Cor 12:6,11).

> They are gifts of grace [and] the gifts of grace (*charismata*) lead to ready, courteous service (*diakonia*). Through the powers of the Spirit...the one Spirit gives every individual [a] specific calling, what is exactly cut out for [them], in the process of the new creation.[129]

The text says that tongues of fire came to 'rest' on each person

— as if the fire sat with them comfortably, burning brightly but not dangerously, generating more light than heat. There is a suggestion here that if people go with their 'burning desire' to become the person that God created them to be, that it will not lead to burnout. Burnout comes not from being too 'fired up', but from being fired up about an abstract ideal or an heroic image of ourselves rather than the reality — limits as well as prospects — of who we are meant to be.

Parker Palmer writes — from painful personal experience — that 'burnout does not come from giving too much, but from trying to give what we do not have to begin with…liberation of society comes not from those who try to change society, but from those who try to be their true selves.' It is Parker's view that the sustainable spiritual dynamic for liberation takes place at the intersection of where our true selves engage the real world around about us.[130]

§

Pentecost shows us that where people are filled with a burning desire to engage the real world in the light of their true selves, they are able to relate to their world with a much greater degree of sensitivity.

In his classic book on the Holy Spirit, *The Go-Between God*, John Taylor writes that the Spirit is the inspiration we all need to engage reality, create true community, make responsible choices and take compassionate actions.

Taylor observes that it is not for nothing that we refer to the world of the spirit as the *nouminous*: 'The word *'numinous'* comes from the Latin *nuo*, to nod or beckon (with a nod). The truly numinous experience occurs when something ordinary as a sleeping child (in the arms of its mother) suddenly commands our attention (beckons us with a nod)'[131] and we can behold the significance of the obvious. 'To be in-the-Spirit is to be vividly aware of everything the moment contains.' The Spirit presents all reality to us, so that it comes to us, strikes us, commands our attention, and we are face to face with the truth of it — not merely the truth about it.[132]

We may often refer to the 'fellowship of the Holy Spirit' (2 Cor 13:14), but Taylor tells us that we seldom recognise how significant the role of the Spirit is to that fellowship:

> the fellowship is the result which we can feel. What causes the fellowship is the gift of awareness which opens our eyes to one another…The Holy Spirit [is] the elemental energy of communion itself, within which all separate existences may be present and personal to each other.[133]

In Taylor's words, the Spirit is not merely the 'ground of our being' but the 'ground of our meeting'. The Spirit turns all our 'we's into one another's'.[134]

Taylor describes an incident where a West Indian woman in London had just got the news that her husband had been killed in a street accident. Apparently she sat on the sofa in the corner of her flat, totally paralysed by the trauma. The teacher of one of her children came by and sat down beside her, put her arm across her shoulders and held her tightly. As Taylor tells it:

> A woman in a London flat was told of her husband's death in a street accident. The shock of grief stunned her like a blow, she sank into a corner of the sofa and sat there rigid and unhearing. For a long time her terrible tranced look continued to embarrass the family…Then the schoolteacher of one of her children…called…and sat down beside her. Without a word she threw an arm around the tight shoulders, clasping them with her full strength. (One cheek touched the other). Then as the unrelenting pain seeped through to her the newcomer's tears began to flow, falling on their two hands…For a long time that is all that was happening. And then at last the [widow] began to sob. Still not a word was spoken and after a little while the visitor got up and went… That is the embrace of God, the kiss of life. That is the embrace of [God's] mission and of our intercession. And the Holy Spirit is the force in the straining muscles of an arm, the film of sweat between pressed cheeks, the mingled wetness of the backs of clasped hands.[135]

It is this love — birthed in our hearts by the Spirit — that becomes the foundation on which people can envisage building the communities of our dreams.

§

Filled with the Spirit at Pentecost, a whole range of people demonstrated an extraordinary degree of *sensitivity* by speaking publicly, from the depths of their soul, about their deepest experiences of community in the past and their deepest hopes for community in the future. By speaking about their visions of community in the language of their hearers' hearts, they were able to create a sense of community with their hearers — even as they spoke!

My mate Paul Tyson says that 'Pentecost is the redemptive inverse of Babel'. Babel was an attempt to build a central global political economy, based on technology rather than morality, using a single universal common language. Pentecost is an attempt to develop a global community of local communities, that are decentralized — not centralized — but empowered by the Spirit to relate to people in all sorts of different languages with the same kind of sensitivity.

When the Spirit came at Pentecost, this vision of community became a reality. Two separate accounts describe with great excitement the exceptionally inclusive, completely egalitarian community that began to emerge post-Pentecost.

> They devoted themselves to the apostles' teaching and to fellowship, to the breaking of bread and the prayers. Awe came upon everyone, because many wonders and signs were being done by the apostles. All who believed were together and had all things in common; they would sell their possessions and goods and distribute the proceeds to all, as any had need. Day by day, as they spent much time together in the temple, they broke bread at home and ate their food with glad and generous hearts, praising God and having the goodwill of all the people. And day by day the Lord added to their number those who were being saved. (Acts 2:42–47)

> Now the whole group of those who believed were of one heart and soul, and no one claimed private ownership of any possessions, but everything they owned was held in common. With great power the apostles gave their testimony to the resurrection of the Lord Jesus, and great grace was upon them all. There was not a needy person among them, for as many as owned lands or houses sold them and brought the proceeds of what was sold. They laid it at the apostles' feet, and it was distributed to each as any had need (Acts 4:32–35).

This is an not an exclusive Christian community, but an inclusive Christ-like community, committed to the way of Christ as a way of relating respectfully to all people regardless of religion, tradition, status, class, caste, age or gender. It creates a society — albeit partially and temporarily — in which the grace of God is the order of the day. The people have everything in common, they distribute their resources to anyone according to their need, and consequently, there is no one with an unmet need — 'no needy persons among them!'

B. The Essence Of Unity And Diversity

In the spectrum of social science research, the term 'community' is not only one of the most common, but also one of the most crucial concepts for the welfare of our society. Yet there is a lot of confusion about the meaning of the term. However, it is possible to distinguish three distinctive common elements among the myriad of definitions: a common physical location, mutual social connections, and reciprocal communal interactions.[136]

David Clark suggests that the passionate quality of communal interaction, or what we might call 'the spirit of the community', is the most important component in community. In *Basic Communities* he writes:

> community [is] essentially a sentiment which people have about themselves in relation to themselves: a sentiment expressed in action, but still basically a feeling. People have many feelings, but there are two essentials for the existence

of community: a sense of significance and sense of solidarity. The strength of community within any given group is determined by the degree to which its members experience both a sense of solidarity and a sense of significance within it.[137]

Psychologist M Scott Peck says,

> ...if we are going to use the word 'community' meaningfully we must restrict it to a group of individuals [like those in the Jerusalem community] who have learned to communicate honestly with each other, whose relationships go deeper than their masks of composure, and who have developed some significant commitment to rejoice together, mourn together, delight in each other, make other's conditions our own.[138]

After researching five different intentional communities in depth, sociologist Luther Smith writes:

> ...the primary indicator of communal well-being is that members feel their fellowship approximates the qualities of a caring family. Hardship and failures will be the occasion for creative solution and increased resolve. They do not break the spirit of a community. But loss of mutual respect and steadfast caring strikes a deathblow at the very heart of a community.
>
> ...the prevailing sense of family is not always easy for these communities to determine...Members can have opposing reactions to the same communal realities. Communities thrive when able to create a fellowship not dependent upon conformity, but which encourages members to remain enthusiastically involved even when they disagree with decisions. While decision making may not always reflect a member's [understanding], it must indicate that the member's ideas have been respected.

§

Sociologist Ferdinand Toennies suggests that while the quality of interaction required to produce a 'society' involves only transient, impersonal, uni-dimensional, secondary relationships; the quality of interaction required to produce a 'community' involves permanent, personal, multi-faceted, primary relationships. Toennies thinks that community such as this is probably only possible for people in kinship groups,[139] and social researcher, Robert Putnam, has recently conducted a study that suggests that Toennies may have a point. In a massive new study based on detailed interviews of nearly 30,000 people across America, Putnam discovered that 'the greater the diversity in a community, the fewer people vote and the less they volunteer, the less they give to charity and work on community projects.' Much to his own chagrin, Putnam concedes that 'in the most diverse communities, neighbours trust one another about half as much as they do in the most homogenous settings.'[140]

Quaker community worker, Parker Palmer, argues that the new kind of human community that the Spirit was trying to bring about at Pentecost was, in fact, contingent from the beginning to the end upon the inclusion of 'the stranger':

> The stranger is a central figure in biblical stories, and for a good reason. The spiritual pilgrimage is always taking us into new lands where we are strangers to others and they are strange to us...Even if we stay at home, even if we are not on a conscious pilgrimage, through [a] stranger, we may have something of the unsettling Spirit brought into our domesticated lives.[141]

The Book of Hebrews says: 'Do not neglect to show hospitality to strangers, for by doing that some have entertained angels without knowing it' (Heb 13:2). The reference is to the three strangers depicted in Rublev's Icon that turn up at Abraham and Sarah's tent in Hebron, where they are welcomed and offered refreshment and rest. In return the strangers, who turn out to be angels, tell them that Sarah, who is well past child-bearing age, will bear the child she wants.[142]

'It is no accident,' Palmer says,

> that God is so often represented as a stranger. God is a
> stranger. God persistently challenges conventional truth, and
> upsets the world's way of looking at things…the stranger
> is the bearer of truth…[and] our everyday perceptions and
> assumptions must be shaken by the intrusion of strangeness
> if we are to hear God's word…the stor[y] use[s an] extreme
> example of unexpected truth: an aged woman bearing a
> child. But even with lesser truths we often need the stranger's
> line of vision to help us to see straight.[143]

A group may be blocked by a simple problem which they simply cannot see their way through because they have lived with it so long. However, an outsider can see it, and remedy it, quite easily.

> People who serve as consultants to organisations know how
> often [just] a slight change in angle of vision can open up
> a new truth…This function of the stranger in our lives is
> grounded in a simple fact: truth is a very large matter, and
> requires various angles of vision to be seen in the round for
> what it is.[144]

The experience of the Jerusalem community suggests that that our relationships with strangers can either make — or break — our societies as communities.

Take for example what happened in the community in Jerusalem after Pentecost. To start with, as a community, they had spontaneously begun selling their possessions and goods, giving to anyone as they had need (see Acts 2:42–47). They then set up a structure to do the redistribution a bit more systematically. 'There was not a needy person among them, for as many as owned lands or houses sold them and brought the proceeds of what was sold. They laid it at the apostles' feet, and it was distributed to each as any had need' (Acts 4:34–35). However, it wasn't long before there were complaints that the centralized distribution naturally favoured the majority group — the Hebraic or Hebrew-speaking Jews — over the minority group in the community at that time — the Grecian or Greek-speaking Jews.

So what did they do about it? Well, the text says:

> The Twelve called together the whole community of the disciples and said, 'It is not right that we should neglect the word of God in order to wait at tables. Therefore, friends, select from among yourselves seven men of good standing, full of the Spirit and of wisdom, whom we may appoint to this task, while we, for our part, will devote ourselves to prayer and to serving the word.' What they said pleased the whole community, and they chose Stephen, a man full of faith and the Holy Spirit, together with Philip, Prochorus, Nicanor, Timon, Parmenas, and Nicolaus, a proselyte of Antioch. They had these men stand before the apostles, who prayed and laid their hands on them. (Acts 6:2–6)

Now it is clear this process still has a long way to go before it is completely congruent with the *modus operandi* that the Spirit represents. There is still an obvious gender bias in the proposed solution to the problem. Nevertheless, there are very significant signs of substantial progress. Firstly, the Grecian widows felt free to complain. Secondly, the Hebraic majority heard what they said, took it seriously, acknowledged there was an injustice and agreed to address the issue promptly. Thirdly, the proposed solution to the problem was accepted on the basis that it 'pleased the whole group'. Fourthly, the people elected to supervise the distribution to ensure that the Grecians got a fair go, were — according to the list of the Greek names given — all probably Grecians themselves. This meant that they had all agreed to give the power to the minority to control the distribution of the resources, so they could ensure their right to access for themselves.

This is a great example of community work in progress: a group of people grappling with ongoing issues, slowly but surely working towards a practice of revolutionary self-control that reflects the 'power of the Spirit' in the process. Paul and his co-workers were 'able to accomplish abundantly far more' than one might have imagined they would have (Eph 3:20). They chose the 'things that are not, to reduce to nothing things that are' (1 Cor 1:28). And time and time again they helped 'foolish' people confuse the 'wise', and 'weak' people confound the 'strong' (1 Cor 1:26–27), in their quest to develop radically inclusive and egalitarian communities of faith in the midst of an established religious tradition which had previously disenfranchised them. They succeeded to such an extent that one horrified observer is recorded as saying that 'these people had turned the whole world upside down!' (see Acts17:6).

C. The Soul Of Originality And Ingenuity

I would like to consider five ways in which the communities of the Spirit Paul nurtured were able to turn their world upside down — and inside out — as well!

First of all, these communities chose to follow the 'un-rule-y' Jesus. Jesus didn't call people to 'follow my rules'. He always called them to 'follow me'. And Paul encouraged them to follow in the footsteps of the notoriously 'un-rule-y' Jesus.

Jesus taught his disciples to pick and choose which rules to obey. After all, he told them, 'you weren't made for the rules, the rules were made for you' (see Mk 2:27). Jesus often broke the rules of his society deliberately. He touched untouchables, against the rules, and gave people a break when it was against the rules to do so. Jesus not only the broke the rules of his society, he even tossed out the rule book. Paul said that 'Jesus destroyed the law with its regulations' (see Eph 2:13–15). So for these communities to follow in the steps of the 'un-rule-y' Jesus was to set out on a path of civil disobedience.

Secondly, Paul encouraged communities of the Spirit not to be conformed, but to 'be transformed', and to become an agent of transformation in society (Rom12:2).

Paul said that as far as he was concerned,

> If anyone else has reason to be confident flesh, I have more…
> in regard to the law, a Pharisee…as to righteousness under the law, blameless.
> Yet whatever gains I had, these I have come to regard as loss because of Christ. More than that, I regard everything as loss because of the surpassing value of knowing Christ Jesus my

> Lord. For his sake I have suffered the loss of all things, and I regard them as rubbish, in order that I may gain Christ and be found in him, not having a righteousness of my own that comes from the law, but one that comes through faith in Christ, the righteousness from God based on faith. (Phil 3:4–9)

Paul said he wanted to deconstruct and reconstruct a whole new political, religious, social and cultural reality through faith in the 'un-rule-y' Jesus Christ. 'As many of you as were baptized into Christ have clothed yourselves with Christ. There is no longer Jew or Greek, there is no longer slave or free, there is no longer male and female; for all of you are one in Christ Jesus' (Gal 3:27–28). If that meant destroying the status quo — so be it! 'But God chose what is foolish in the world to shame the wise; God chose what is weak in the world to shame the strong; God chose what is low and despised in the world, things that are not, to reduce to nothing things that are' (1 Cor 1:27–28).

Thirdly, Paul encouraged the communities of the Spirit to always be prepared to ask open questions in the closed political systems that they were a part of.

Community activist, Fran Peavey, comments:

> Questioning is a basic tool for rebellion. It breaks open the hardened shells of the present, and opens up the options that might be explored. Questioning reveals the profound uncertainty that is imbedded deep in all reality beyond the facades of confidence and sureness. It takes this uncertainty towards growth and new possibilities. Questioning can change institutions and entire cultures. It can empower people to create strategies for change.[145]

Paul loved asking questions that undermined the authority of the system and opened up options for people that — until that time — had been considered completely closed.

> If God is for us, who is against us? He who did not withhold his own Son, but gave him up for all of us, will he not with

> him also give us everything else? Who will bring any charge against God's elect? It is God who justifies. Who is to condemn? It is Christ Jesus who died, yes, who was raised, who is at the right hand of God, who indeed intercedes for us. Who will separate us from the love of Christ? Will hardship, or distress, or persecution, or famine, or nakedness, or peril, or sword? (Rom 8:31–35)

The answers Paul canvases are nothing less than revolutionary.

> No, in all these things we are more than conquerors through him who loved us. For I am convinced that neither death, nor life, nor angels, nor rulers, nor things present, nor things to come, nor powers, nor height, nor depth, nor anything else in all creation, will be able to separate us from the love of God in Christ Jesus our Lord. (Rom 8:37–39)

As the activist theologian, Charles Elliott, reminds us, Paul was prepared to:

> Question the right that a system assumes to rule.
> Question the concentration of power assumed in the system.
> Question the tyranny of precedent assumed in the system.
> Question the monopoly of virtue assumed in the system.
> Make sure that each and every system knows that they are answerable for the way that they act, not merely to themselves, but to everyone affected by their activities, particularly those affected adversely by their activities. Call to account those who maintain oppressive structures, reminding them of the need to judge those structures from the standpoint of those who are oppressed (and One who identifies with those who suffer from oppression), rather than from those who benefit (from the oppression).[146]

Fourthly, Paul encouraged the communities of the Spirit to always conduct radical conversations in the conservative societies that they were a part of.

Wherever he went, Paul developed what he called ekklesia. These ekklesia were never defined in terms of vertical relationships — like worship — but in terms of horizontal relationships — as fellowships — 'for one another'. These gatherings were set up as support groups for conversations that could help participants tear down the 'strongholds' of their society (2 Cor 10:3–5) and 'build people up' (see 1 Cor 14:26; Eph 4:11–16).

Mark Strom points out that the process involved in the radical conversations Paul conducted were critical of the conservative societies in which they were conducted. The conversations were open to all people and ranged across the topics of everyday life. Paul's goal in these conversations was to discourage anyone, including himself, from setting themselves up as an authority or accepting any authority — apart from Christ. 'His goal is to induce self-examination and self-criticism in relation to Christ[147]...Christ gave coherence to Paul's conversations. Paul modeled the freedom of Christ. Christ gave new shape to social relations. Each conversation brought grace to some aspect of everyday life, liberating practice from enslaving social conventions.'[148]

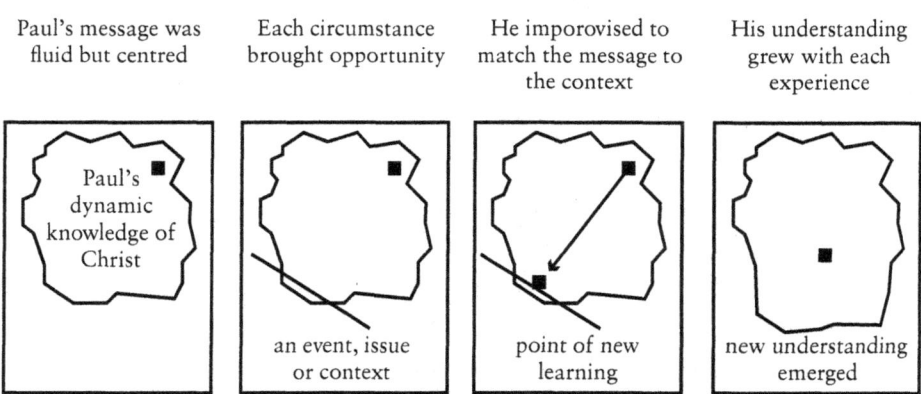

Figure 6: The Radical Christ-Centred Process in Paul's Discussions.[149]

Paul practised a 'dynamic knowledge of Christ' in each situation he encountered (see Box 1 Figure 6). Then he engaged an 'issue' in the 'context' of the situation he encountered in the light of his 'dynamic knowledge of Christ' (see Box 2 Figure 6). Then he experimented with various ways that he could engage an 'issue' he encountered in the light of his 'dynamic knowledge of Christ' (see Box 3 Figure 6). And then evaluated his understanding of various ways he could engage an 'issue' he encountered in the light of his 'dynamic knowledge of Christ' (see Box 4 Figure 6).

Mark Strom also points out the *content* of the radical conversations Paul conducted was thoroughly critical of the conservative societies in which they were conducted (see Table 2).

The Conservative Content of Graeco-Roman Society	The Radical Content in Paul's Discussions
Knowledge in terms of abstraction	Knowledge in terms of stories
Coherence through use of reason	Coherence through the Spirit
Pursuit of the ideal over the real	Pursuit of relations through love
Centering on the ideal of virtue	Centering on the person of Christ
Importance of balance	Importance of abandonment
Celebration of status	Critique of status
Maintenance of the status quo	Change of the status quo
Transmission of social conventions	Transformation of social conventions
Interest in hierarchy	Interest in mutuality
Focus on individual ambition	Focus on community shalom
Value of extraordinary over ordinary	Value of ordinary everyday life

Table 2: The Radical Christ-Centred Content in Paul's Discussions.[150]

Fifthly, Paul encouraged the communities of the Spirit to always seek to develop an alternative culture that subverted the dominant order of the day.

Paul knew that counter-cultural communities that could subvert the dominant order of the day did not need not be large. They could actually be quite small — a group who met in a house was big enough. The issue for Paul, as it was for Jesus, was not the size of the group, but the Spirit of the group, and the way that the group allowed the Spirit to embody in them a Christ-like social reality.

> For just as the body is one and has many members, and all the members of the body, though many, are one body, so it is with Christ. For in the one Spirit we were all baptized into one body — whether Jews or Greeks, slaves or free...God has so arranged the body, giving the greater honour to the inferior member, that there may be no dissension within the body, but the members may have the same care for one another. If one member suffers, all suffer together with it; if one member is honoured, all rejoice together with it. (1 Cor 12:12–13; 24–26)

The communities of the Spirit that Paul nurtured turned society upside-down and inside-out — they brought diverse groups together in unity, gave greater honour to those who usually got less and practised equality with one another.

PART THREE

AN IMAGINATIVE METHOD FOR COMMUNITY DEVELOPMENT

A. HEARING OUR CALL TO BE 'ECCLESIA'

Religious congregations can be very effective agents of community in society. Most congregations are more or less self-supporting entities. They are usually one of the first community agencies local people establish, and one of the few community agencies that last in depressed, and depressing, neighbourhoods — long after the banks have gone. Congregations typically provide a context for mutual support.

All major religions teach responsibility for one another, including the stranger. They all teach the need to help people regardless of social status, and they all provide models of compassion. Congregations of people from all major religions create groups in which there are social expectations of reciprocity, social norms, rewards and sanctions around the practice of reciprocity, and the development of intricate sets of social obligations that can be counted upon.[151]

Connections For Life, a study conducted in 2002 by Peter Kaldor, Keith Castle and Robert Dixon on behalf of the National Church Life Survey, showed that church-attenders are more likely to be involved voluntarily in community activities than non-attenders.[152] In fact, church attendance is a greater predictor of volunteering than education level, and volunteering increases with church attendance, both for individuals and their families.[153]

Kaldor et al. observe that 'the size of this volunteer workforce is huge, with hundreds of thousands of people making a regular commitment of time and energy. Their investment in society shouldn't be underestimated or undervalued.' In Australia, 30 percent of local churches are currently providing up to 50 percent of the self-help groups in their local community, 40 percent of them are providing personal counselling, and 60 percent of them are providing material assistance. Furthermore, large church and para-church agencies are by far the biggest non-government providers of social services, including family welfare, child care, youth work, aged care, disability support and employment services.[154]

Robert Putnam writes that in countries like the US, local churches are:

> ...arguably the single most important repository of social capital...as a rule of thumb, our evidence shows, that half of all philanthropy (or charity) is religious in character, and half of all volunteering occurs in a religious context...American religious communities spend roughly US$15–20 billion annually on social services. Nationwide in 1998 nearly 60 per cent of all congregations reported contributing to social service, community development or neighbourhood projects; 33 per cent support food programs for the hungry; and 18 per cent support housing programs [for the homeless]...Black churches have been prominent in recent efforts to rebuild inner-city communities.[155]

I think the magnificent contribution that churches and other faith-based community groups make to society is often overlooked in a resolutely secular society such as Australia. I can remember going some years ago to an award ceremony for community volunteers at state parliament. It was a very special occasion for our family, because my father-in-law, as being given a government award for 50 years of community service to 'new Australians'. As I watched the proceedings with great interest, I noticed that out of the dozen volunteers who were given awards that day, for decades of selfless service to migrant and refugees, at least nine were actually church-based volunteers. But their faith — which had been so obviously such a significant common factor in their commitment to volunteering — never got a mention.

However, when it comes to commitment to involvement in community activities, not all is as healthy on the faith-based community front as some claim.

Firstly, while interest in religion continues, interest in religious institutions like the church is on the decline. Those churches not on decline tend to be more inward-looking than outward-looking, and their members are more likely to be involved in the church than in the locality, or in church activities in the locality.[156]

Secondly, many growing churches have opted for large regional models rather than small local models of church growth. The larger the congregation is, the less likely it is for its members to be involved in local community activities. They are more likely to be involved in in-house at-church activities.[157]

Thirdly, the people involved in a lot of in-house at-church activities are increasingly out of touch with their local communities. A recent survey reported that 21 percent of people in church said they still had contact with more than ten people in their locality for more than fifteen minutes per week. However, 23 percent of people in church said they only had contact with only one or two people in the locality — and 16 percent had no contact all![158]

Fourthly, as people in churches have less contact with their local communities, they have less commitment to involvement with their local communities. A recent survey reported that 28 percent of people in church said they were involved in serving people outside the church in a local group or organisation. However, 72 percent of people in church said that they weren't involved in a local community group or organisation in any capacity at all![159]

§

If the church is going to be an effective agent of community development, we need to *change our idea of church*. I was taught that the key to understanding the church was the Greek word ecclesia, which we translate into English as the word 'church'. This is the word used by Jesus when he said in Matthew 16:18, 'I will build my church, and the gates of Hades will not prevail against it.' I was taught that ecclesia here meant 'called out'. So the church was really those called out of the society, apart from the society, to stand for the truth against the false values of the society, in the hope that even the forces of hell itself would not prevail against it.

This definition of the 'church' is essentially separate. It sees church as not only apart from the society, but also 'over against the society'. It is this separate idea of church that still affects the way many of us see the place of the church — or the temple, mosque or synagogue — in the society: at a respectable distance from society. So the church contributes to society through religious agencies, congregational activities and congregants' occupations. However, society is still kept at a respectable distance. As we have seen in the survey data we just cited, 42 percent of people in churches said they had little contact with people in the locality, and 72 percent said they weren't involved in serving people in their locality outside the church at all.

However, when Jesus first used the word *ecclesia*, it was not a religious term. It was a political term referring to a community council — people in a locality who were called aside, for a while, to consider how to promote the welfare of their locality. The church — or the temple, mosque or synagogue — was not intended to be those who were 'called out of the society'. The church was called to be 'in it', but 'not of it'. Not *apart from* the society, but *a part of* the society, promoting its welfare. Not fighting against flesh and blood, but against the powers — including their own religious 'powers' — in the society that oppress people.

This definition of church is essentially *connected*. It sees church — or the temple, mosque or synagogue — as a part of the society working for the welfare of the society. To connect with society, the church needs to move from *bonding* to *bridging*. *Bonding* involves developing strong inward-looking connections, or bonds, like marriage, that of necessity are exclusive. Bonds produce deep, 'thick' trust, and are essential for nurturing and supporting one another, for 'getting by'. Churches — with our emphasis on family — generally do bonding better than bridging (see Figure 7A). *Bridging* involves developing weak outward-looking connections, or *bridges*, like the civil rights movement that of necessity are inclusive. *Bridges* produce broad, 'thin trust', and are crucial for co-operating and campaigning with others — for 'getting on'. Churches, with our suspicion of others who are not considered to be brothers or sisters in the family of faith, do not generally do bridging very well (see Figure 7B). We need to continue to *bond* with people of the same beliefs in our churches, but not at the expense of building *bridges* to other people in our communities with different beliefs from ourselves.[160]

A. BONDING   B. BRIDGING

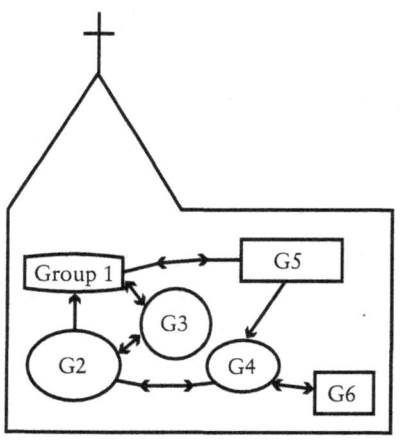
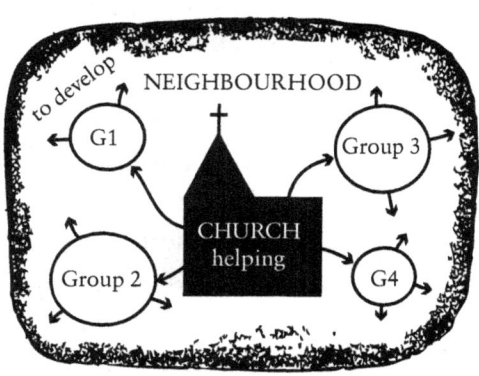

Figure 7: To connect with society, the church needs to move from *bonding* to *bridging*. A. *Bonding* involves developing inward-looking connections.[161] B. *Bridging* involves developing outward-looking connections.[162]

§

The trinity should not only be our *model* of community, but also our *modus operandi* for community development. Jesus sent his disciples out into localities, 'two by two', Lk 10:1) to look for a third person, the 'person of peace', (Lk 10:6) with whom the disciples could 'stay'(Lk 10:7) and form a trinity as the key building block for creating 'trey' communities .

Those of us who are religious need to note that the indicator Jesus gave to his disciples to discern who they should work with was a spiritual descriptor, a 'person of peace' — open, responsive, compassionate, helpful' — *not* a religious descriptor. The 'person of peace' we need to look for may be an adherent of any religion — or none.

Trinitarian or 'trey-way' community work involves triangles and triangulation. According to Richard Buckminster Fuller, humble *triangles* are among the most 'energetic-synergetic constructions', or 'energy-synergy efficient structures', that there are in the world. Using triangles, Buckminster Fuller created his 'Geodesic Dome', a home shaped like a half of a sphere, that proved to be extraordinarily strong, in spite of having no internal or external supports at all.[163] *Triangulation* is the division of a surface into a set of triangles. Every surface has a triangulation. We can use the triangulation of a surface for navigation.[164] The Global Position System (GPS) is a type of navigation based on a global positioning system of triangulation that is sophisticated enough to give us our altitude, speed and an accurate position on planet Earth.[165]

'Trey-way' community work involves developing *networks of triangles* with at least three men and/or women of 'peace'. Just as we use our GPS to assess our altitude, speed and position on Earth by *triangulation*, we can assess our community development in the light of the network of 'trey' relationships, or interpersonal triangulation, we have with people dedicated to a spirit of compassion.

'Trey-way' interpersonal triangulation with men and women of peace not only enables us to position ourselves in terms of community development, *it also enhances our capacity to make the most of our position* — through a phenomenon that Tom Atlee calls 'co-intelligence'. Atlee defines co-intelligence, or 'connected intelligence', as the ability to generate creative responses and initiatives that integrate the diverse gifts of all for the benefit of all.[166]

Co-intelligence functions through multi-nodal and multi-modal intelligence. *Multi-nodal* intelligence means there is more than one intelligence in play. *Multi-modal intelligence* means there is more than *one type* of intelligence in play. In a trey-way community network, there is always more than one person involved and each one brings their own unique kind of intelligence to the table. Co-intelligence functions collectively and collaboratively.

A trey-way community network has the potential to function not just as a set of individuals, but as a collective family, group or organisation — indeed, as a whole living system. As a collective, it has the potential to find other collectives, and form alliances with other families, groups and organisations, collaborating as 'parts of a greater whole' for the benefit of all living things. Atlee describes co-intelligence as being 'attuned to life' and able to evoke 'a deeper intelligence in and around it'. Thus, the practice of co-intelligence is very resonant. It 'deepens our empathic response to life, enabling us to resonate with other sources of intelligence, both human and divine. Co-intelligence helps us to sense an intelligent Presence in and round us and find the guidance that is there.[167]

Trey way interpersonal triangulation — and the connected intelligence it creates — is so vital to the task of authentic community development, that Jesus told his disciples if they could not find a third person to triangulate with in a locality, they should move on and look elsewhere (see Lk 10:1-9).

It takes one person to make an 'individual'. It takes two people to make a 'couple'. It takes at least three people to make a 'community'. Where there is an individual, there is an 'I' with zero (0) relationship. Where there is couple, there is an 'I-You' with one (1) relationship between two people. Where there is a community there is an 'I-You-We' with at least three (3) relationships between at least three people (see Figure 8). A true community is a 'trey'.[168]

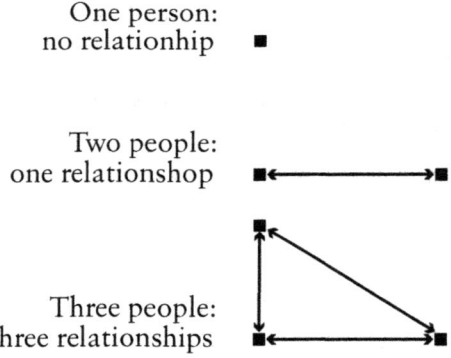

Figure 8: The number of relationships possible involving up to three people.

A 'trey' creates the *stability* and *security* that is essential for community. If the relationship between two people is strained, in a threesome the relationship that the two people have with the third can hold the community together (see Figure 9).

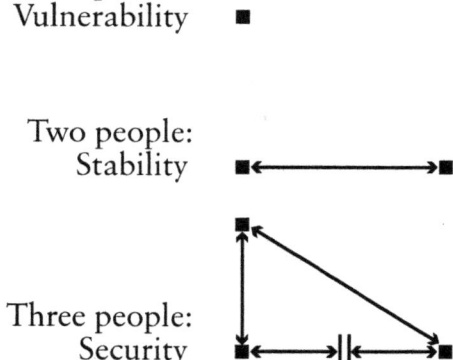

Figure 9: At least three people are needed in order to create stability and security

A 'trey' creates the *subjectivity* and *objectivity* essential for community. If there is a problem in a relationship between two people, in a threesome the problem can be understood subjectively by each of the two people involved and understood more objectively by the third person, who can act as a witness (see Figure 10).

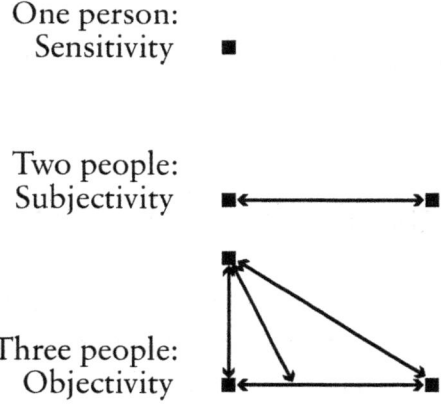

Figure 10: At least three people are needed to create subjectivity and objectivity.

Finally, a 'trey' creates the possibility of developing a community that can embody the extraordinary love of God revealed in the Trinity. One person can make a spiritual point about the love of God. Two people can draw a theological line with regard to the love of God.

However, it takes three people to create a trinitarian space that can embody the counter-cultural love of God in society (see Figure 11).

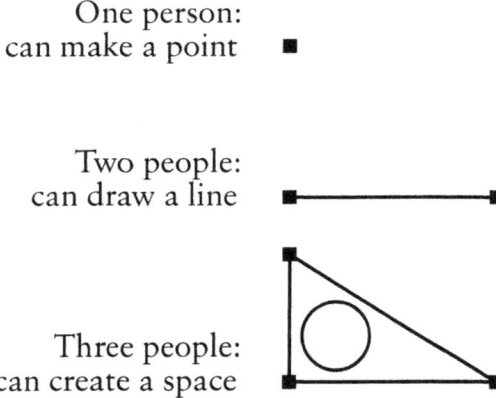

Figure 11: At least three people are needed to create a the space for community.

People can *hear* something of God's love when a single person talks about it. They can *see* something of God's love when a couple of people relate tenderly to one other. But they can *feel* something of God's love when they step into a community of people which embody God's love and *they experience it themselves as part of the community.*

B. SEEING OUR SELVES AS 'YEAST IN THE DOUGH'

If the church is going to be an effective agent of community development, we need to *change our image of church*. I used to see church as 'the light of the world'. It was to be a 'city of virtue set high on top of a hill' shining brightly for the whole world to see. This image tends to reflect and reinforce the idea of the church as 'apart from society'. We need to find an image that help us see the church not as *apart* from the society, but as *a part* of the society and promoting its welfare.

I found what I was looking for in the Parable of the Yeast. Jesus said that: 'The kingdom of heaven is like yeast that a woman took and mixed into [a large amount] of flour until it worked all through the dough' (Mt 13:33). When I found this image I realised that, as modest as it was, it was in fact a very significant image that had the potential to not only reframe the role of the church, but also restore its reputation in the community. For the purposes of our discussion, I'd like to suggest we see the church as the 'yeast' and the community as the 'dough'. Note that the yeast only does its work when it is mixed into the flour to such a degree that you cannot tell the difference between the yeast and the flour. It is then, and only then, that it makes a difference. And what is the difference that it makes? It causes the whole (cultural) milieu, into which it has been mixed, to rise!

Now, there are two time-honoured ways of mixing with people in the community that the Jews refer to in Yiddish as *schmoozing* and *maching*. *Schmoozing* is an informal approach to mixing. *Schmoozers* like to visit family, drop in on friends, invite newcomers over for a barbecue, or take old-timers out on a picnic. *Maching* is a more formal approach to mixing. *Machers* are more likely to attend a workshop on community, start a community group and implement a community project. Interestingly, the distinction between *schmoozers* and *machers* not only reflects different personalities, but also different stages in the life cycle. Putnam observes that *schmoozing* 'peaks among young adults, enters a long decline as family and community obligations press in, then rises again with retirement...[while *maching*] is relatively modest early in life, peaks in late middle age, and declines with retirement'.[169] Most of the time we tend to be mainly one or the other. However, to mix well, we need to be a bit of both. We need to take an *informal* approach to mixing by visiting family, dropping in on friends, inviting new-comers over for a picnic, and taking old-timers out on a barbecue; and we need to take a *formal* approach to mixing by attending seminars on community, starting community organisations, and implementing community projects.

We don't all have to do it the same way. Different people will play different roles at different times. However, whatever we choose to do will be but a beginning in the long, slow process of mixing that will slowly but surely ferment change in the community — *developing the relationships that will raise the quality of the life of our community.*

In order to develop relationships that will raise the quality of the life of our community, we need to make sure that we develop relationships on a trinitarian basis.

The temptation for us when we take an informal approach, and play the role of a *schmoozer* in the community, is that we will operate 'charismatically' and build relationships centred on ourselves. This is a very attractive option for many of us, as it makes us the centre of attention — the star of our very own show. However, it does not create a healthy community, as it makes the group dependent on us, rather than interdependent. Furthermore, as the group is dependent on a star, and stars are inclined to 'crash and burn', or simply 'burn out', it is very unstable.

The temptation for us when we take a formal approach, and play the role of a *macher* in the community, is that we will operate 'institutionally' and build relationships based on an organisation. This is also a very attractive option for many of us, as it means we can create an institution that will last long after we have gone. But again, it does not create a healthy community. It may create a more stable community, but at the same time it also creates a more impersonal community, where relationships are defined in terms of roles, rules and regulations.

If we want to raise the quality of the life of our community, we need to resist the temptation to opt for either the charismatic or the institutional approach, no matter how attractive they may be, or how articulate their advocates may be. We can only develop the healthy, stable, interdependent, personal relationships that will raise the quality of the life of our community, if we make sure we practise 'trey-way community work' as *schmoozers* and *machers*, and develop relationships with people built on trinitarian relational dynamics (see Figure 12).

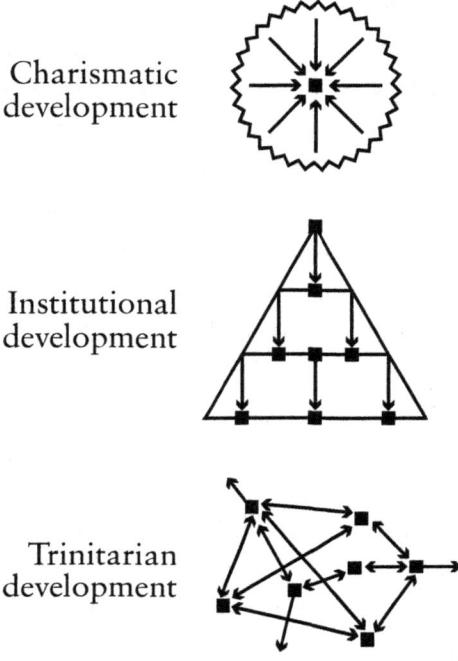

Figure 12: Three different approaches to development. The Charismatic and Institutional approaches serve the community. But only the Trinitarian approach can create community.

§

The test of the quality of life of our community is in how strangers experience it.

Community is where strangers can meet one another on common ground. The most basic function of community is to help us recognise and adjust to the fact that our lives are fundamentally interconnected with strangers. In our families we do not usually connect with strangers as such. We would generally only invite strangers into our homes if we wanted to make friends with them. But in our communities we connect with strangers as such constantly. We meet strangers on the street who we will never become friends every day of our lives. And it is there we learn to share our lives with strangers as well as friends.[170]

Community is where fear of strangers can be acknowledged and dealt with. In our families we only learn to deal with people who are 'like us' — people who speak the same language, with the same religion, from the same background. So we become more confident in relating to people 'like us' and less confident in relating to people who are not 'like us'. Many of us actually become afraid of dealing with 'the other'. So we live in private homes, travel by private transport and study at private schools. We pay insurance, so if we are sick, we are vouched safe beds in a private hospitals. It is only in our communities that we learn deal with people who are not 'like us' — people who do not speak the same language, do not have the same religion, and are not from the same background. Travelling on public transport on the way to a public event, and afterwards having a meal together with 'others' in a 'pub' (an abbreviation of 'public house') can increase our confidence in dealing with strangers.[171]

Community is where our resources can be generated and shared. The problem of how to share scarce resources is a basic problem that needs to be solved in every society. If we do not solve this problem in a way that benefits everybody, then we might have a reason to be afraid that somebody else is going to attack us and take what we've got. However, everyday we walk on a public footpath in rush hour, we have the opportunity to learn how to share a scarce resource — in this case space — with strangers in a way that benefits everybody.[172]

Community is where conflicts can be generated and resolved. Conflicts are a part of life. But because of the 'stranger danger' campaigns that we run in our society, people are particularly scared of conflicts with strangers. 'Road rage' crimes are spectacular. So they often get a lot of media attention. They may not happen a lot. But because of a lot of attention they get, people think they happen a lot. And they're scared to go out on the roads. But every time we are driving in a car with our children, and we stop to allow somebody to walk across the road on a pedestrian crossing, we can teach our kids about the possibility of sharing the road happily with others.[173]

Community is where life can be given texture, colour, and drama. In our homes we are familiar with everything. But once we step out of our homes we step into a world that is where everything is fascinating. If we walk along the South Bank parkland by the Brisbane River we encounter a world of colour — in the crowds of multi-ethnic people in brightly coloured clothes promenading on the walkways under the arches of red bougainvillea, dressed in everything from quiet white hijabs and sedate black kaftans to loud orange tank tops and busy silver lycra shorts. If we sit in one of the coffee shops on the footpath in West End, we encounter a world of drama — in the bubbly yuppie customers chatting excitedly at a table nearby, and the world weary Big Issue vendor with a poignant story to tell passing slowly by on the street. These encounters allow us to move beyond fear to fascination with the other. Indeed these random events, mingling with strangers, gives rise to 'a kind of human electricity'.[174]

Community is where people can be drawn out of themselves. Many individuals are self-centred. And many of our families are either a collection of self-centred individuals or a collective form of self-centredness. But when we encounter others in our community we are confronted with the fact that the world does not revolve around us and our family. We will be forced to respond to others one way or another.[175]

Community is where mutual support can become a real possibility. When we encounter the poor, the sick and the broken people around us, we are faced with a choice. Do we acknowledge we are related to one another and accept that we have a responsibility to use our time and energy and resources to help them — or not? In an authentic community 'we encounter the poor, the sick, the broken, [and] the more able among us [can] develop a deeper sense of our need to assist our less able brothers and sisters'. We 'come in contact with one another — and learn to care for one another'.[176]

Community is where opinions can become audible and accountable. In private we can say what we like — and usually get away with it. No matter how erroneous or dangerous or damaging what we say is to others. But when we speak out on a topic in public, strangers who may have a different opinion may well dispute what we say. We are far less likely to get away with saying things that are erroneous or dangerous or damaging to others. In community our opinions are scrutinised and criticised.[177]

Community is where people can be both empowered and protected.

It is only by moving from the private to the public domain that that people can have an impact on the government — and, when necessary, protect themselves from the government. Community gives people the opportunity to grow in the confidence and acquire the skills that are required to engage the world around about them actively, creatively and constructively. In community we develop the capacity to organise effectively.[178]

Community is where visions can be projected and projects attempted. Visions may be conceived in private, but can only be birthed in public. A painting needs to be seen. A poem needs to be heard. And a new social reality can only become a reality in society. As it did on the day of Pentecost.[179]

The stranger is the one who constantly tests the quality of our community life. Parker Palmer writes that 'the stranger is not simply an individual, but one who represents an entire class of people who are pressed to the bottom layer of our world.' He continues, '[Christ says that] the viewpoint of the stranger not only affords a fuller look at the world; but a deeper look at ourselves, our own lives' from his perspective.[180] Jesus illustrates this in his parable of the sheep and the goats (Mt 25:31–46), which speaks of the welcome he has received from the righteous. The puzzled righteous respond:

> 'Lord, when was it that we saw you hungry and gave you food, or thirsty and gave you something to drink? And when was it that we saw you a stranger and welcomed you, or naked and gave you clothing?'...And the King will answer them, 'Truly I tell you, just as you did it to one of the least of these who are members of my family, you did it to me.' (Mt 25:37–38, 40)

Palmer argues that it is not the private realm, but the public realm, in the community 'where strangers meet', that is the 'final proving ground for faith'. 'In every encounter with a stranger we are given a chance to meet the living Christ. If we turn our back on "the least of these" we turn our back on God — and on our own true selves.'[181] However, if we embrace the stranger, we can embrace God's vision of 'true' community for us and for our world.

C. ACTING AS 'LITTLE BROTHERS AND SISTERS OF JESUS'

If the church is going to be an effective agent of community development, we need to *change our model of church*. When I was young I was brought up to try to be 'a *great* man of God'. As William Carey, a famous Baptist missionary, said: to 'expect *great* things from God; to attempt *great* things for God.'[182] Hence, I was always looking for something *great* to do. However, one day I was confronted with the example of Jesus. The approach practised by Jesus was not *great*. To the contrary, it involved consciously setting aside any aspirations that he may have had to *greatness*. In addition, Paul says, those of us who would follow the example of Jesus need to empty ourselves of our ambition to do *big* things — so that we can do *little* things *with a lot of love over the long haul — as little brothers and sisters of Jesus* — who was prepared to empty himself of all his privileges and make himself a mere mortal (see Phil 2:1–8).

As I've said before, Christ moved in alongside us, as one of us. He did not try to be different. He lived the same life that other people lived, experiencing the same hassles and the same hardships as everybody else. Christ wasn't full of himself. Rather, emptying himself, he immersed himself in the lives of others, allowing their concerns to fill his consciousness. In the midst of their common struggle, Christ made himself available to the people as their servant, seeking in all he said and did to set them free to live their lives to the full. When it came to the crunch, Christ did not cut and run. He was prepared to pay the price for his commitment to people — in blood, sweat, and tears.

Taking the approach Christ took is not something we can do vicariously through others. It is something we must do ourselves. There is a role for organisations, as they may provide a useful framework for the work we want to do in the community. There is also a role for professionals, as they may provide extra insight, knowledge, and skill that is useful for increasing the effectiveness of the work we want to do. However, there is simply no substitute for our face-to-face, hands-on, grass-roots involvement. If we're going to get involved like Christ did, we've got to step out into the community and get our hands dirty too.

The first step is to move into a community. We must be willing to set aside our concerns for security and status. We must be willing to forgo the comforts that privilege and position bring, in order to meet people, many of whom are profoundly disadvantaged and distressed, on their territory and on their terms. *The second step is to remember our humanity.* We must not try to be different from the people around us, but discover the similarities we share in the humanity that runs as blood through our veins. We all get sick. We all get tired. We all grow old. Nevertheless, we all want to love and be loved. And we all want to live life to the full before we die. We can share these common struggles with our brothers and sisters in the community — even if our economics, politics, culture, and religion are poles apart. *The third step is to empty ourselves.* We must empty ourselves of our preoccupation with our own thoughts and feelings so that we can immerse ourselves in the lives of others and allow their joy and their anguish to fill our lives. *The fourth step is to serve others.* We must enter into people's struggles with them, and, in the context of that struggle, serve them as a servant — not like a public servant, but like a personal servant. Our relationships with people should be marked by an uncommon quality of care; a quality of life that reflects the love of Christ, who came 'not to be served, but to serve, and to give his life as the price he was willing to pay' (see Mt 20:28) to bring life to people in the community. *The fifth step is to embrace suffering.* If we are going to have any hope of bringing life to people in our community, we too must be willing to pay the price, by dying to ourselves in the midst of the inevitable frustrations, tensions, difficulties and conflicts that work in the community always entails.

There is no easy option. If there were, Christ would have taken it. He was a messiah, not a masochist. Christ took the hard path because it was the only path that he could take that would lead to the practice of compassion. So, for those of us who would follow in his footsteps, there is no other way than to open our heart and risk the heartache and the heartbreak of real involvement in peoples' lives. Compassion comes from 'com' meaning 'with', and 'passion' meaning 'suffering', so to practise compassion means being willing to suffer with others, like Christ did.

If I were to ask you what you thought was the hardest step for you to take, all of you would no doubt have different replies. But I would like to suggest that I know of no step more difficult for us to take in our acquisitive capitalist society than the third step in the process — the middle step, or the central step — the step of emptying ourselves and making time and space in our lives for others.

One thing we need to empty ourselves of is — seeking success. As part of the great consumer generation, we all tend to be more preoccupied with materialistic rather and non-materialistic values, like appearance, finance and success. Radicals have as many difficulties with these things as conservatives; they are just preoccupied with different versions of the same thing! They want to be like Mother Teresa rather than Maggie Thatcher, or Mahatma Gandhi rather than George Bush. However, we all tend to be preoccupied — positively or negatively — with body image, private property, and public recognition. We need to empty ourselves of our preoccupation with materialism and make room for the Spirit.

A second thing we need to empty ourselves of is — playing games. We may try to empty ourselves of materialistic values and embrace more non-materialistic values, like personal development, social responsibilities, and communal contributions. However, we are often still so influenced by the materialistic perspective of our culture that we all still tend to give our spiritual acceptance, relationships and connections a heavy-handed materialistic twist. This perspective leads to the 'objectification' of people, turning our relationships with 'people' into relationships with 'things', and using them as a means to attain our ends. Materialistic people tend to develop 'instrumental friendships' which are characterised by a low degree of empathy, a high degree of manipulation, and a willingness to disclose truth only when it is useful. This leads to a lot of game playing. We all know the rules of the games we play: keep the conversation shallow, but pretend it is deep; talk about yourself, but tune out when others talk about themselves; use meaningful jargon, but avoid a genuine meeting of souls. Two of the favourite games of those of us who are conservative are the *piety game* and the *proselytisation game*, and two of the favourite games of those of us who are radical are the *ideology game* and the *indoctrination game*. The object of the piety game and the ideology game is to convince others and ourselves of our virtue. Both the piety game and the ideology game are characterised by judging people on the basis of our pet issues. They are not concerned about meeting people at their point of need. It is about using their needs to make them look bad, and make us look good by comparison, and prevents a genuine encounter in which we can come to terms with our common needs together. The object of the proselytisation game and the indoctrination game is to convince as many people as possible to join our cause. In both the proselytisation game and the indoctrination game, we treat people as faceless commodities — potential trophies for us to win. We do not treat people as people. If we meet people's needs, it is not so much to help them win, but to help us win them over. Both the proselytisation game and the indoctrination game may promote encounters with people, but they will subvert the possibility of developing relationships of mutual acceptance and respect. Christ refused to play games. He criticised people who played piety and ideology games (Mt 23:23), as well as proselytisation and indoctrination games (Mt 23:15). He condemned those who pretended to be concerned for the welfare of others when their only concern was for themselves (Mt 23:25). He consistently called for a *genuine* concern for others. Hence, *Christ calls us to empty ourselves of everything — but love.*

A third thing we need to empty ourselves of is — wasting time. If we want to relate to people in our locality we need to *live* in our locality. We need to empty ourselves of our tendency to live our lives everywhere else but where we are located. If we want to relate to people in our locality we need to not only *live* in our locality, but *stay* in our locality. People who expect to move in five years are 25 percent less likely to get involved in their locality. If we want to get more involved, we need to stay around for more than five years. To do that, we need to empty ourselves of our tendency to keep on the move. If we want to relate to people in our locality, we need to spend less time at *church* and more time in our locality. If we reduce involvement in church to three meetings — a large celebratory gathering, a small nurture group, and a small action group — then we will have more time for locality. To do that we will need to empty ourselves of our preoccupation with church. If we want to relate to people in our locality we need to spend less time at *work* and more time in our locality. Two-career, full-time working households are less likely to be involved, but part-time work is more likely to increase community involvement for both women and men alike.[183] To increase our involvement we will need to empty ourselves of our preoccupation with career-orientated full-time work. If we want to relate to people in our locality, we need to spend less time *commuting* and more time *communicating*. Every ten minutes not spent in commuting increases the possibility of community involvement by 10 percent — not only of the commuters, but those associated with them.[184] If we want to spend more time *communicating*, we need to stop watching *Neighbours* and start relating to neighbours. Though those who watch the news on television are more likely to be involved in the community than those who do not, those who watch talk shows, game shows and soap operas are less likely to be involved in the community.[185] TV takes time[186], induces passivity[187] and provides a sense of pseudo-community[188]. Consequently, each extra hour a day of watching TV reduces community involvement by 10 percent.[189] *One of the easiest ways to make time for community is to turn off the TV!*

So we turn off the TV — *where* do we start? The answer to the question is — start *wherever* we are! Start right here — right now — wherever we are! Maybe we could start with contacting some of the people around us. Let's just make sure we resist the temptation of going for either the *great* charismatic approach or the *great* institutional approach. For, as we know, we can only develop the healthy, stable, interdependent, personal relationships that will increase the quality of the connections in our community, if we practise the *not-so-great* 'trey-way community work' approach and develop relationships with people that are built on humble, mutual, trinitarian relational dynamics.

We need to remember that in taking the initiative to contact people, we can make connections with people; but, it is only as we seek to connect each person with at least two others, and they form networks of at least three persons in reciprocal relationship with one another, that they will be able to begin to experience the true liberating quality of non-controlling trey community (see Figure 13).

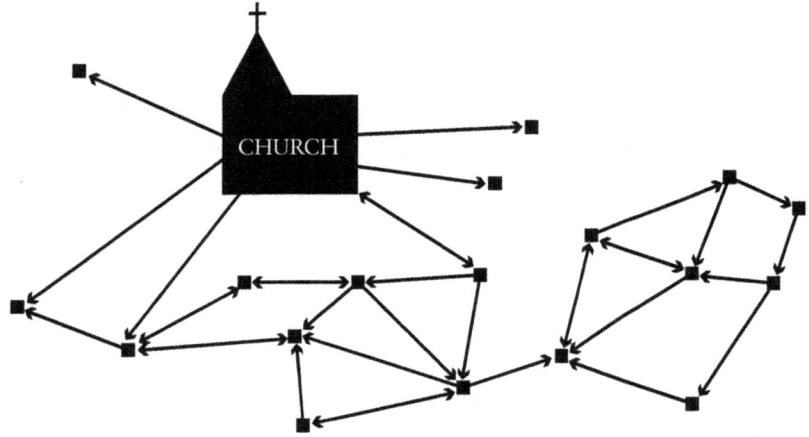

Figure 13: Trey relationships in the community outside the church.[190]

However, we can only create the space for non-controlling trey community to develop, if we empty ourselves of our desire to control others, give up playing power games, and relate to people with genuine trinitarian care and concern.

Similarly, our temples, mosques and synagogues; municipal, provincial and federal authorities; and local, national and international agencies will only be able to create the space for non-controlling trey community to develop in their areas of concern, if they empty themselves of their desire to control others, give up playing their power games, and relate to people with genuine trinitarian care (see Figure 14).

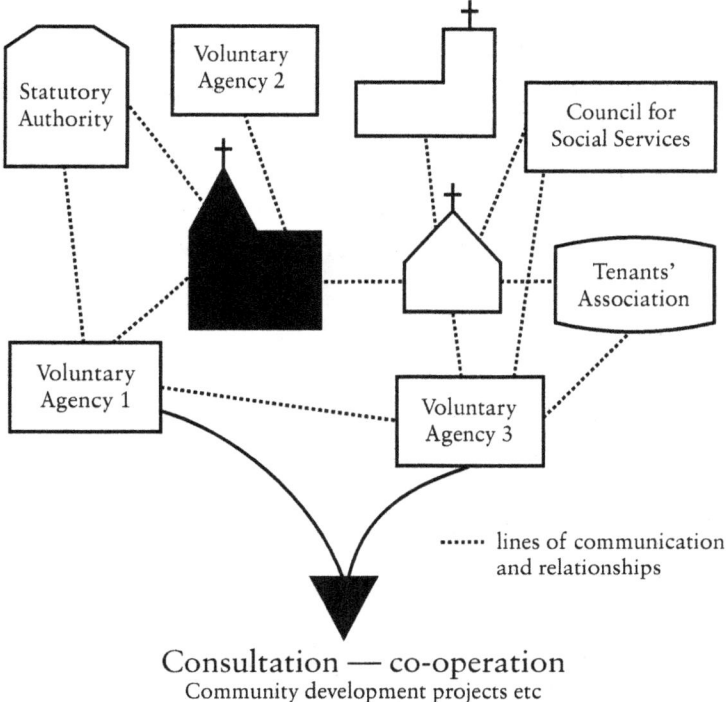

Figure 14: Trey relationships with local, national and international groups and agencies.[191]

After all, as the eminent British community development work scholar, George Lovell, reminds us, when all is said and done 'community development means working for the growth of each individual, group, and organisation, and for the establishment of healthy interdependent relationships between them.'[192]

D. TURNING OUR WORLD 'UPSIDE DOWN AND INSIDE OUT'

The first time we meet Paul in the Bible, he is supervising the stoning of the Stephen (Acts 7:54–8:1) — whom the apostles saw as a gracious man, full of the Holy Spirit, (Acts 6:5) — but whom Saul, the Pharisee, saw as a dangerous blasphemer who needed to be publicly executed as soon as possible (Acts 6:11). However, on the road to Damascus, Paul was personally confronted by the 'once-dead-now-risen' revolutionary Jesus, who pointed out to him that to oppress people working for Christ-like change was to oppress Christ himself (Acts 9:3–5). For Saul, that realization meant everything had to change! So he and his friends took their whole world to task, and set out to reshape it, bit-by-bit, according to the upside-down inside-out values of Jesus Christ of Nazareth.

Paul's plan for turning his world upside-down and inside-out consisted of five key components: a passion for transformation, attention to preparation, a sensible long-term strategy, practical short-term tactics, and blood, sweat and tears.

i. A Passion for Transformation

Paul's plan was based on a passionate commitment to transformation:

> I appeal to you therefore, brothers and sisters, by the mercies
> of God, to present your bodies as a living sacrifice, holy and
> acceptable to God, which is your spiritual worship. Do not be
> conformed to this world, but be transformed by the renewing
> of your minds, so that you may discern what is the will of
> God — what is good and acceptable and perfect.
> (Rom 12:1–2)

For Paul, being transformed, being a subject and agent of transformation — as opposed to being conformed to the current secular and religious patterns of operation in the world — was his *spiritual mission, his way of worshipping God.*

As we have already seen, Paul had a clear vision of the kind of transformed communities that he wanted to see:

> Let love be genuine; hate what is evil, hold fast to what is
> good; love one another with mutual affection; outdo one
> another in showing honour. Do not lag in zeal, be ardent in
> spirit, serve the Lord. Rejoice in hope, be patient in suffering,
> persevere in prayer. Contribute to the needs of the saints;

> extend hospitality to strangers.
> Bless those who persecute you; bless and do not curse them.
> Rejoice with those who rejoice; weep with those who weep.
> Live in harmony with one another; do not be haughty, but associate with the lowly; do not claim to be wiser than you are. Do not repay anyone evil for evil, but take thought for what is noble in the sight of all. If it is possible, so far as it depends on you, live peaceably with all ...
> If your enemies are hungry, feed them; if they are thirsty, give them something to drink...Do not be overcome by evil, but overcome evil with good. (Rom 12:9–18; 20–21)

If we are going turn our world upside-down and inside-out like Paul, we need to be fired by the same passion for the same vision for transformation as he was. However, we need to remember, Paul did not only have a *passionate* commitment, but he also had a *practical* commitment to transformation.

As a conservative, Paul knew how resistant and reactive people could be to change. He had had change agents — Jesus' followers — beaten up and thrown into prison, and had personally supervised the public stoning of Stephen (Acts 7:54–8:1). So when he was advising Jesus' disciples, Paul urged them to proceed with great caution.

Paul quickly followed his call for them 'to present [their] bodies as a living sacrifice' in the service of transformation which is pleasing to God (Rom 12:1), with his call for them to conform — by submitting themselves to the authorities as much as they could — without compromising their commitment to transformation (Rom 13:1–7).

There are probably many reasons Paul gave them this advice, but I can think of a couple of very important practical reasons why he did so.

On the one hand, Paul was convinced that if they *did not conform*, or 'submit' to some degree, they would quickly provoke the wrath of the authorities, who — he warned them — did not 'bear the sword for no reason'! (Rom 13: 1–4). Paul himself had experienced 'far more imprisonments, with countless floggings, and often near death. Five times I have received from the Jews the forty lashes minus one. Three times I was beaten with rods. Once I received a stoning...' (2 Cor 11:23–25).

On the other hand, Paul was convinced that if they *did conform*, or 'submit' to some degree, people would take their adjustment and their accommodation as a sign of 'respect' and be more likely to reciprocate (Rom 13:7).

> For though I am free with respect to all, I have made myself a slave to all, so that I might win more of them...To those under the law I became as one under the law (though I myself am not under the law) so that I might win those under the law...I have become all things to all people, so that I might by any means save some. (1 Cor 9:19–20, 22)

So, once we have decided to work for the transformation of an organisation, Paul tells us that we need to proceed with care, conforming to the requirements of the institution as much as we can, while reserving the right to refuse to conform to any requirement which is contrary to 'the law of love' (see Rom 13:8).

Because we refuse to conform to anything contrary to our conscience, we are ultimately a threat to any institution which depends on the conformity of its members for its survival. But, because we are willing to do everything we can to conform, the institution does not immediately perceive us as a threat or treat us as a threat. This gives us time to work towards a change.

However, we must always remember that the change we seek is not Machiavellian but Pauline, and is committed to 'do what is right in the eyes of everybody'.

ii. Attention to Preparation

The first step Paul took in working for change was to seek a *sponsor*. Paul's sponsors included people like Priscilla and Aquila, whom he stayed with and worked with, and who introduced him to the synagogue in Corinth (Acts 18:1–3) and saved his skin when he got into trouble! (Rom 16:3).

A *sponsor* is person in an organisation who *empathises* with us and who is *willing to give us a bit of space to work for change*. It doesn't have to be a lot of space. Even a little space can make a lot of difference, as it can give us room to move in an environment that would otherwise restrict our movements. For a sponsor to be effective, he or she needs to be in a position within the organisation to not only provide us with space, but also protect that space. If we can't find an effective sponsor, our chances of success are close to zero.

Being a Baptist, the first local church I went to when I moved into where I live was a Baptist Church. However, I was unable to find anyone in the church who was the least bit interested in the kinds of things that I wanted to do. So I tried the next church nearest my house. It was an Anglican Church that went by the auspicious name of 'St Andrew's'. When I met the minister, I knew I had found the sponsor that I was looking for. His name was John. He'd lived in Pakistan at the same time we'd lived in India, and we both spoke Urdu. Like Ange and I, John wanted to develop the inclusive kind of church community that the subcontinent teaches people is so vitally important, and so we joined St Andrew's.

The second step Paul took was to find at least a couple of *supporters*. Paul's supporters included people like Barnabas, Mark, Silas and Luke. These people publicly supported Paul in his campaign to change the world. They set out on the great adventure together, risked the hazards of the road, argued about the route they should take, went their separate ways, got back together again, and shared the joys and sorrows of the grand endeavor — outlined in the book of Acts.

A *sponsor* is person in a group who *empathises* with us and who is *willing to give us a space to work for change*. A *supporter* is a person who *sympathises* with us and who is *willing to join us — wholeheartedly — in our work for change*.

For a sponsor to be effective, he or she needs to be in a position within the organisation to not only provide us with space, but also protect that space. For a supporter to be effective, he or she needs to share our pain about the closed nature of the system, and be willing to help us in trying to open it up. Whereas we need to only find one sponsor in a group to get a bit of space; we need to find at least two other supporters to develop a trey counter-culture.

When we decided to get involved with St Andrew's, Chris and Ruth and Nigel and Sue decided to get involved with us. We quickly developed a rapport with a whole range of people already involved in the church, like Jeremy, Betti, Tim and Sue and Norma. This network was big enough for us to begin our own DIY church reformation.

iii. Sensible Long-Term Strategy

The most common way of trying to change an organisation has always been to mobilise a group of disenfranchised and disaffected people at the bottom to overthrow the people at the top, and thereby institute a change of regime. This can be done either violently, by revolution, or non-violently, by election.

Either way, the more things change, the more they stay the same, because no matter how many times you may change the regime, the system remains (see Figure 15).

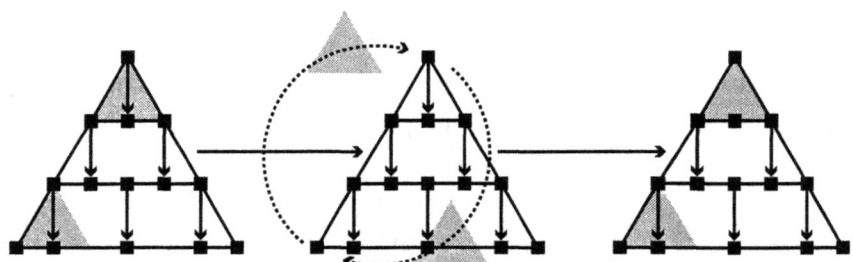

Figure 15: Regime change — those in charge may change, but the system remains the same.

Paul's approach was based on Jesus' much more innovative, alternative strategy — *of not trying to change the regime, but the system itself.*

Jesus' strategy was simply to persistently deny hierarchy, advocate mutuality, and reframe all his relationships, over time, in terms of equality. Over and over again, Jesus told the people who were with him to reject any kind of hierarchical *modus operandi*, and embrace the practice of mutuality.

Jesus said:

> You know that the rulers of the Gentiles lord it over them, and their great ones are tyrants over them. It will not be so among you; but whoever wishes to be great among you must be your servant…just as the Son of Man came not to be served but to serve, and to give his life a ransom for many. (Mt 20:25–28)

> But you are not to be called rabbi, for you have one teacher, and you are all students. And call no one your father on earth, for you have one Father — the one in heaven…The greatest among you will be your servant. All who exalt themselves will be humbled, and all who humble themselves will be exalted. (Mt 23:8–9, 11–12)

To start with, the disciples related to Jesus as their 'Rabbi', but over time he reframed his relationship with all of them in clear, radically egalitarian terms. After three years, he said to them: 'I do not call you servants any longer, because the servant does not know what the master is doing; but I have called you friends, because I have made known to you everything that I have heard from my Father' (Jn 15:15).

Paul took on Jesus' strategy and made it his own. He denied hierarchy, advocated mutuality, and reframed relationships in terms of equality.[193] He told the church at Galatia that he believed all people were equal in Christ: 'There is neither Jew nor Gentile, neither slave nor free, neither male nor female, for you are all one in Christ Jesus' (Gal 3:28). When Paul wrote a letter on behalf of Onesimus, an escaped slave, to Philemon, his former master, he asked Philemon to welcome Onesimus back, 'no longer as a slave, but as you would welcome me, as a dear brother':

> I am appealing to you for my child, Onesimus, whose father I have become during my imprisonment. Formerly he was useless to you, but now he is indeed useful both to you and to me. I am sending him, that is, my own heart, back to you. I

wanted to keep him with me, so that he might be of service to me in your place during my imprisonment for the gospel; but I preferred to do nothing without your consent, in order that your good deed might be voluntary and not something forced. Perhaps this is the reason he was separated from you for a while, so that you might have him back for forever, no longer as a slave but as more than a slave, a beloved brother — especially to me but how much more to you, both in the flesh and in the Lord.
So if you consider me your partner, welcome him as you would welcome me. If he has wronged you in any way, or owes you anything, charge that to my account.
(Philem 1:10–18)

Paul's strategy for change in the synagogue did not involve mobilizing the slaves against the masters. Rather it was to undermine the hierarchy itself by building up mutuality, and — very carefully — reframing inequality in terms of equality, one relationship at a time (Figure 16).

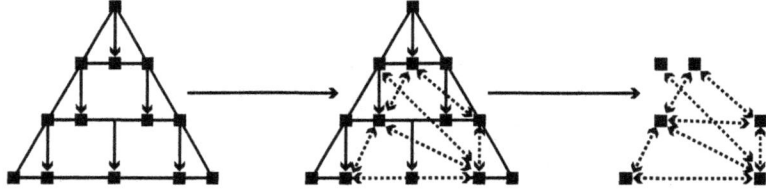

Figure 16: Paul's strategy for change: reframing the hierarchy in terms of equality.

The kind of changes that we need involve system change, rather than regime change. Therefore, rather than spend all our time fighting the current regime, we need to be working slowly but surely for transformation of the entire system — by implementing Paul's strategy of white-anting hierarchy, building up mutuality, and reframing the inequality in terms of equality, one relationship at a time.

The first relationship at St Andrew's that I started on was my relationship with the 'rector'. Even though the word 'rector' meant that he was the 'ruler' — and by implication that framed our relationship in hierarchical terms: he was the 'ruler' and I was the 'ruled' — I didn't react to the title. I simply ignored it. I related to John as a person as respectfully as I could, and when John moved on and Alan replaced him, I treated Alan the same way. In order to reframe the relationship in terms of equality, I used to ask Alan out to have a coffee in a local coffee shop, which was away from his office, where he was the 'pastor' and I was the 'parishioner'. In the coffee shop, we were just 'a couple of middle-aged men', and as we shared our joys and sorrows over a cuppa, we became good friends. We noticed that when we became friends, the dynamics of the interaction between us and our friends began to change. There was a greater degree of trust, and that made everyone feel a little safer. There was also a little more acceptance and respect. People felt that if they spoke, they would be heard, and they could shape decisions that were being made. This relational change led to organisational change.

iv. Practical Short-Term Tactics

When people at the bottom of an organisation feel powerless, they think that if only they were able to work their way to the top of the organisation they would be in a position to have the power to bring about the change that they desire (see Figure 17).

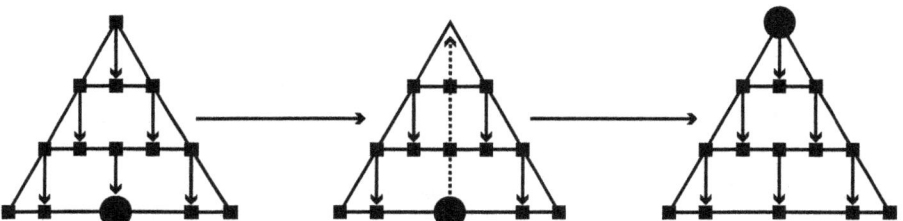

Figure 17: Moving from bottom to top to be in a position to impose top-down change

However, many of those who have reached the top of an organisation claim that people at the top are as constrained by the structure as people at the bottom. Although I believe that may be an overstatement, I do think there is undoubtedly some truth in it.

Paul, certainly, did not encourage anybody to work their way from the bottom to the top of any system they happened to find themselves in: 'Everyone should remain in the situation which they were in when God called them' (1 Cor 7:20). He said: 'Were you a slave when you were called? Don't let it trouble you ...' (1 Cor 7:21a). Then added, rather enigmatically, 'although if you can gain your freedom, do so' (1 Cor 7:20–21).

On the surface, this seems typical of Paul's advice — a bit of a contradiction! No wonder Peter said 'his letters contain some things that are hard to understand' (1 Pet 3:16). Ain't that the truth!

However, if we go a little deeper, we will discover that there is more to this contradiction than immediately meets the eye. On the one hand, he is counseling people not to move up in the system; on the other hand, he is counseling them to gain their freedom if they can. So, where — we need to ask — does Paul expect people — oppressed by the system — to find freedom from oppression, without moving up in the system? I think the only answer is — by *moving out!*

Paul encouraged everybody not to move from the bottom to the top. Paul encouraged people to move from the centre to the edge of any system that they found themselves in. Again, in this regard, Paul based his approach on a strategy of Jesus'.

Jesus publicly associated with the synagogue, to the extent of participating, 'as was his custom', in congregational meetings (Lk 4:16). However, he didn't attempt to move up in the organization, choosing instead to move to the outer edge of the institution. This location 'on the side-lines', rather than 'in the main game', gave him some great advantages.

First of all, it gave him *perspective*. From the sidelines he was able to see the whole field, and see what needed to be done to improve the game. Second, it gave him *opportunity*. On the sidelines he was far enough away from the game to be beyond its immediate control, yet close enough to affect the way it played out. Third, it gave him *time*. On the sidelines he was able to develop his short-term alternatives to the system while he worked on his long-term transformation of the system. Fourth, it gave him *space*. On the sidelines he was able to demonstrate the alternatives he developed in the eyes of everyone, so they could assess for themselves whether they wanted to adopt them — or not. Fifth, it gave him a *position from which he could advocate change*, without being in a position to impose the change he advocated on anyone. So people knew they were truly free to adopt the change — or not to — as they so desired. Furthermore, because that made the change process much less threatening to the people in the synagogue, *it gave Jesus greater freedom* to experiment more!

Paul adopted the same strategy that Jesus used concerning the synagogue. Rather than attempting to move up in the organization of the synagogue, he moved to the edge of the system, developing alternatives people were free to accept, if they succeeded — or free to reject, if they failed.

Paul's trade as a tentmaker was crucial to his strategy. It was his occupation when he was 'called', and he stuck with it, just as he had advised others to do (Acts 18:3; 1 Cor 7:20–21). As a position, it was low in status. However, it was a self-supporting profession that gave Paul a high degree of independence, 'out on the cutting edge of society', and he used it to develop his *ecclesia* — the communities of his dreams.

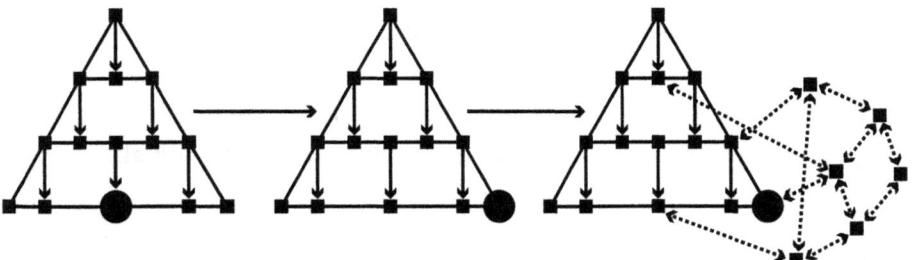

Figure 18: Moving from the centre to the edge to incarnate the change advocated

In these experimental groups, Paul worked side by side with slaves, ate and drank with 'clean' and 'unclean' alike, and encouraged the people around him to 'live in harmony with one another' (Rom 12:16).

Paul did everything he could to make his experimental communities:

A safe space —

> ...extend hospitality...If it is possible, so far as it depends on you, live peaceably with all. (Rom 12:13,18)

where a person was accepted as a person;

> Let love be genuine...love one another with mutual affection; outdo one another in showing honour. (Rom 12:9–10)

where unity and diversity were respected;

> ...we, who are many, are one body in Christ, and individually we are members one of another. We have gifts that differ according to the grace given to us...(Rom 12:5–6)

where no-one was treated as unimportant;

> ...outdo one another in showing honour...do not be haughty, but associate with the lowly...(Rom 12:10, 16)

where everyone was taken into account;

> ...take thought for what is noble in the sight of all. If it is possible, so far as it depends on you, live peaceably with all. (Rom 12:17–18)

and where there was a commitment to do justice — regardless.

> Contribute to the needs of the saints; extend hospitality to strangers...Do not repay anyone evil for evil...If your enemies are hungry, feed them; if they are thirsty, give them a drink...Do not be overcome by evil, but overcome evil with good. (Rom 12:13, 17, 21)

Paul's prayer was that his experiments would not stay 'on the margins', but that his *ecclesia* would become 'the centre of attention', not only to be admired, but also to be adopted as the *modus operandi* of society.

Paul wrote to the communities of his day,

> I appeal to you...be imitators of me. (1 Cor 4:16)

> For you yourselves know how you ought to imitate us; we were not idle when we were with you...with toil and labour we worked night and day, so that we might not burden any of you. This was...in order to give you an example to imitate. (2 Thess 3:7–9)

> Be imitators of me, as I am of Christ. (1 Cor 11:1)

> If then there is any encouragement in Christ, any consolation from love, any sharing in the Spirit, any compassion and sympathy, make my joy complete: be of the same mind, having the same love, being in full accord and of one mind. Do nothing from selfish ambition or conceit, but in humility regard others as better than yourselves. Let each of you look not to your own interests, but to the interests of others. Let the same mind be in you that was in Christ Jesus...
> (Phil 2:1–3)

Paul worked for the day when synagogues would adopt the *modus operandi* of his *ecclesia* and would develop into transformed communities.

The kind of change I hoped and prayed for at St Andrew's was that we would become a transformed community — safe, accepting and respectful; where everyone would be treated as special, no matter how dysfunctional their behaviour was; and everyone could participate in decisions about matters that were important to them.

Our long term strategy was to foster mutuality and reframe the inequality in terms of equality, one relationship at a time. But long term change nearly always takes a long time. So we also had a go at carrying out short-term changes by moving out to the edge, developing some creative alternatives, and waiting for the right moment to bring our experiments back from the margins into the very centre of congregational life.

A few of our friends had already had a go at bringing about change by joining the parish council, and trying to influence the direction of the church through its formal decision-making procedures. However, they felt blocked at every turn by precedents and protocol, and became so disheartened that they finally left the church in despair. So Ange and I, and our friends, decided to explore the possibilities of experimenting with some community involvement — not as part of a formal church programme, but as an informal community response. Although our experiment would be associated with the church, it wasn't to be run by the church; we were far enough from the church so as not to be a threat, but close enough to be a potential catalyst for change.

We began visiting isolated people in our area. We talked to them, and listened to them tell us something of their modest aspirations — like getting out of the hostel every now and again, and having a nice meal with some friends. As a result of these discussions, we decided to start what we called a 'community meal'.

Right from the start, the community meal was a shared meal. In fact, some people call the 'community meal' the 'share meal'. The term indicated the idea that the meal was not a *welfare* event, where others provide for us, but a *friendship* event, where we provide for one another. Those who had a lot were encouraged to bring a lot. Those who had a little were encouraged to bring a little. But everybody was encouraged to bring something along for the meal. Some people used to bring casseroles in crock pots. Others would bring a few tea bags, or a small milk carton. Still others would check out the rubbish bins on the way, and bring whatever treasures they could find…

When there was just a few of us, we used to meet in someone's house. As time went on, however, the numbers of people who dropped in for dinner grew, and we had to move into a community centre. Over the next three years, some fifty to a hundred people used to gather every fortnight, on a Friday night, at the House Of Freedom.

The community meal was a party to which everyone was welcome, no matter how badly dressed, or badly distressed. As such, it became a party for everyone in the area who was left off everyone else's party list — including some of the most wonderfully fragile and freaked-out characters in the inner city.

The people who came appreciated the community meal so much that they'd plan for the next one as soon as the last one was over. Older women would get a new rinse, on special at the local hairdressing salon. Older men would get a new suit from the local op shop. Young punks would sport their fashionable, but savagely misnamed, safety pins, poked through the flesh on various parts of their anatomy. When we got together, we probably looked like a sideshow, but we always looked upon one another as friends. We shared not only the latest neighbourhood gossip, but also some of the deepest parts of our selves, the best kept secrets of our lives.

When an ABC television crew were doing a documentary on St Andrew's — based on the undeniable beauty of its building — the church suggested a special segment on the community meal. And when the documentary on St. Andrew's featured the community meal as part of the church programme, it represented the moment that our informal experiment was formally adopted by St Andrew's. A little while later we asked if we could move the community meal onto the church premises, and our request was granted. Some would say that since that day, St Andrew's has never been the same again. (See Figure 19)

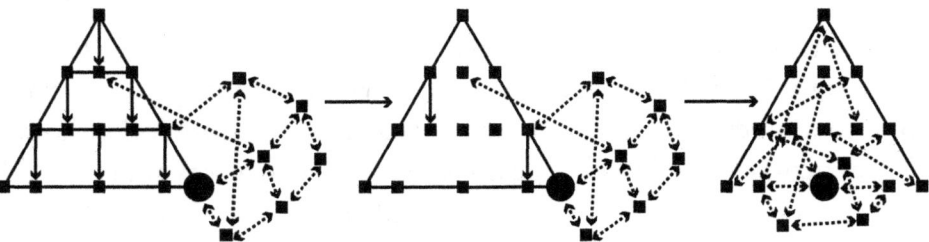

Figure 19: Moving from the edge back to the centre incarnating change in the system

Now, many people think there is no point working for change on the margins. However, I think that there is often no other place where we can work for change, until there is a *kairos* moment — an opportune moment — of some kind or other, which can open up a closed system. Such a moment, of which the ABC documentary featuring the community meal is an example, can give us a chance to take the changes we have accomplished on the margins, and place them — for serious consideration — right at the heart of the organisation. It doesn't matter whether the *kairos* moment comes sooner or later. *What does matter is that we recognise it when it comes, and use it to advocate the kind of change that can facilitate the development of a healthy community.* Whether the crisis be conflict in the group, criticism of the organisation, or a succession in the leadership, we can use it to encourage people to consider serious change.

Ange and I continued to attend St Andrew's for quite a few years before we saw any significant change. Then one day our minister came to see me. He was scheduled to go away on sabbatical, but had no priest to replace him, so he enquired whether a friend and I would take over the evening service in his absence. Seeing this as an opportunity to bring some of the changes we had been involved with on the periphery into the centre of the church, my friend and I indicated our willingness to take on the job, as long as we could turn the service into a church event that the people coming to the community meal would feel comfortable with. Our minister was more than happy with that, as he was concerned that the church not only provide a space for people to have a meal, but a place for people to be at home.

So with his approval, we began to transform the service, from a fairly rigid form that very few people in the community could relate to, into a much more relaxed format that made people feel at home. We particularly tried to change the service in such a way that it could be more meaningful to some of the people with physical, intellectual, and psychiatric disabilities that we knew. The service became more personal and more relational, inviting participation and tolerating interruptions. We made it more simple and more practical, raising issues and sharing responses. And we tried to make it more inspiring and more empowering, by not only by praying, but also partying together at church.

When our minister returned from his sabbatical, I'm sure he couldn't believe his eyes to begin with. Instead of six, there were over sixty people at the service, 30 percent of whom had a serious disability, but all of whom were 100 percent involved in the event, singing and dancing along with the everybody else. Needless to say, had our minister not supported the change, it would have been difficult, if not impossible, for it to be sustained. However, in spite of his misgivings over certain matters — which he spoke to us about, and which we did our best to take into account — he gave the change his blessing, and let the revolution roll on.

The significance of such a transformation should not be discounted. Churches can be notoriously hierarchical, patriarchal, patronising, and domesticating. It's almost impossible for some people to imagine a church that is really mutual, equitable, egalitarian, and liberating. Yet, that's exactly the miracle that I see with my own eyes each week at St Andrew's!

Every Sunday night, our community gathers in the basement of the church. People amble in, in dribs and drabs. Gradually, a large motley crowd from around the neighbourhood forms into a large multilayered circle of humanity. The people that come don't leave their problems at the door. We know our problems are as welcome as we are, so we come with our distress, depression, neuroses, psychoses and schizophrenia, in the hope that, together, we can reaffirm our significance as people over and above our problems.

We begin by lighting a candle, to remind us of the radiance of hope that we have, which shines in the midst of our despair. This sounds very wonderful, but it is often the occasion for a furore, as different people fight for the right to light the candle. Having settled that dispute, some have so much difficulty in lighting the candle without burning themselves, that they burst into a sustained bout of profanity as the service begins.

Like other churches, we enjoy singing together; however, when we do sing, it's like no other church I know. Some of the people that come just love to sing their favourite songs, and demand that we sing them every time we meet. Once Brad gets started, no one can stop him.

He's a human juke box, with no 'off' switch and an endless supply of songs. Some of the people that come can neither hear nor speak, but pick up on the vibes when we sing; running to and fro, they make whatever noises they can, in order to join in. Ron got into clapping so much once, that he didn't quit for the rest of the night. He clapped right through the songs, the sermon, the passing of the peace and the closing prayers. Everyone is encouraged to participate in the service, on the assumption that everyone, regardless of our disability, has a contribution to make through the service to one another's lives.

The first time Sally led the service, she sat in a back seat and spoke so quietly that no one knew what was going on. The second time she led the service, she actually sat at the front where everyone could see her, but no one could hear her. The third time, she not only sat at the front, where everyone could see her, but also spoke loud enough for everyone to hear her.

I can never forget the time Kate and Jane took the service. They are both solo mothers who have suffered the indignity of having their children taken away from them by government authorities, and as a consequence, have felt quite suicidal at times. Yet, never has the gospel been more faithfully proclaimed in that church than it was the night that Kate and Jane spoke. The good news, according to Kate and Jane, is that 'though we may be treated like shit, and be tempted to feel like shit, we're not shit. For the love of God can make us feel as if we're as good as gold — as good as gold!'

Through the change at work at St Andrews, the locality is coming to church and the church is becoming a community. People are finding the confidence to be themselves and realise their amazing potential as men and women made in the image of God. To me, it's a touch of heaven on earth...

v. Blood, Sweat and Tears

We need to remember that there is usually no gain without pain. The struggle for transformation is typically saturated with blood, sweat, and tears. In a strange but poignant turn of phrase, Paul again speaks of the suffering he has experienced as a transformation agent: 'I am now rejoicing in my sufferings for your sake, and in my flesh I am completing what is lacking in Christ's afflictions for the sake of his body, that is, the church' (Col 1:24). So it should come as no surprise that bringing change to our churches often involves a sacrifice of blood, sweat, and tears, shed for the sake of Christ's body — the people meant to embody community love in society.

Because of the grace of key people, working for change at St Andrews has been relatively painless. However, in that regard, our experience at St Andrews is not typical; over the years, our work for change has met with a lot more failure than success. Along the way, I've been scolded, censured and sacked, rebuked, physically assaulted, tossed out on the street, and excommunicated. It is not surprising that some people like Gordon Preece, the editor of *Zadok Perspectives*, publicly refer to me as a 'Jeremiah' — 'a weeping, often angry, prophet'. He may be right.

§

Reflecting on my own painful experience as a wanna-be trey-way change agent, I have come up with my very own 'Change Agent Pain Scale' (see Table 3).

Change Agent Pain Scale	
Level One	Disturbing
Level Two	Distressing
Level Three	Devastating

Table 3: Change Agent Pain Scale

Let me describe three levels of pain I have experienced in working for change. Your experiences may have been similar.

Level One: Disturbing

The last time that I spoke in a church in my home town 25 percent of the congregation walked out. After the service, of the 75 percent of those who stayed who hear what I had to say, only two people would speak to me — a friend of a friend and a visitor.

Level Two: Distressing

I used to teach a course on Christian community work at the Queensland Baptist College of Ministries. However, someone made a complaint about the content of the course. An enquiry was held. And though I thought that I acquitted myself quite well, I was not invited back to teach another course at the college for more than ten years.

I used to work for Queensland Baptist Care and though the Director of Queensland Baptist Care said the training we provided under their auspices was regarded as excellent, the funding for our programs was cut, the property we used to run our programs was sold, and all the staff in our training unit was retrenched.

Level Three: Devastating

I used to be a part of a small-is-beautiful, hands-on, grass-roots, local community ministry called Dilaram, that was taken over by a global evangelistic agency known as YWAM (Youth With A Mission). I was very concerned about the YWAM-ification of Dilaram, and decided to speak out against it. But — when I spoke out against YWAM I became a marked man. Leaders from YWAM, flew into town, from the four corners of the compass, to make sure that they dealt with me. They said I was a 'rebel', and as 'a rebel', I should be summarily excommunicated. So promptly expelled me from the community.

From that moment on, I was no longer allowed to be part of the community that, up until then, had been my whole life. My wife and I and our young child were literally put out of our home and not permitted to return — not even to pick up my luggage. Lest anyone talk to me. And, of course, everyone was forbidden to either talk with me or offer me any help. Those who did so risked the same treatment themselves, so few did.

In the ensuing days I tried to talk with people, but, sadly, even people who had been my friends, who saw me coming down the street, would turn their back on me and simply walk away. I was devastated that people I respected wouldn't even give me the time of day. Instead, would precipitously pitch me and my family out of our home; dump my wife and I, with a young child, out in the street; and, then ban everybody in the community — on pain of excommunication — from helping us. *All in the name of the Lord!*

No one was more honest about the pain involved in such a process than Paul. He had experienced

> ...far more imprisonments, with countless floggings, and often near death. Five times I received from the Jews the forty lashes minus one. Three times I was beaten with rods, once I received a stoning. Three times I was shipwrecked; for a night and a day I was adrift at sea; on frequent journeys, in danger from rivers, danger from bandits, danger from my own people, danger from Gentiles, danger in the city, danger in the wilderness, danger at sea, danger from false brothers and sisters, in toil and hardship, through many a sleepless night, hungry and thirsty, often without food, cold and naked. And, besides other things, I am under daily pressure because of my anxiety for all the churches. Who is weak, and I am not weak? Who is made to stumble, and I am not indignant?
> (2 Cor 11:23–26)

Yet, somehow, Paul was able to absorb the pain without it destroying him. 'We are afflicted in every way, but not crushed; perplexed, but not driven to despair; persecuted, but not forsaken; struck down, but not destroyed' (2 Cor 4:8–9).

How did Paul manage to take the punishment without being crippled by it?

§

Paul had to quickly develop his very own 'Emergency Plan For Acute Pain' (see Table 4).

An Emergency Plan for Acute Pain	
Step One	Run
Step Two	Hide
Step Three	Die
Step Four	Rise
Step Five	Try Again

Table 4: An Emergency Plan for Acute Pain.

Step One: Run

We think of Paul as a heroic figure who stood his ground. But Paul knew that, at times, it was better to run than to stand your ground.

> ...the Jews plotted to kill him, but their plot became known to Saul. They were watching the gates day and night so that they might kill him; but his disciples took him by night and let him down through an opening in the wall, lowering him in a basket. (Acts 9:23–25)

At this point, Paul ran away.

Step Two: Hide

As well as being prepared to run away, Paul was also prepared to stay away for years at a time — hiding from the risk of further harm. 'Then I went into the regions of Syria and Cilicia, and I was still unknown by sight ... Then after fourteen years, I went up again to Jerusalem...' (Gal 1:21–2:1).

Step Three: Die

When Paul was hurt he cried, and sometimes the hurt was so great that he wrote to his friends that he felt like he was actually 'dying' inside:

> [We are] always carrying in the body the death of Jesus, so that the life of Jesus may also be made visible in our bodies. For while we live, we are always being given up to death for

Jesus' sake, so that the life of Jesus may be made visible in our mortal flesh. So death is at work in us, but life in you. (2 Cor 4:10–12)

Step Four: Rise
Although Paul often felt like he was 'dying' inside, he also said that, in Christ, he found the strength to live on and to 'rise' to the next occasion: '…as servants of God we have commended ourselves in every way…We are treated…as dying, and see — we are alive; as punished, and yet not killed; as sorrowful, yet always rejoicing' (2 Cor 6:4, 8–10), 'I can do all things through [Christ] who strengthens me' (Phil 4:13).

Step Five: Try Again
Time and time again Paul overcame acute existential pain to try and try again. 'We who are alive are always being given over to death for Jesus' sake, so his life may also be revealed in our mortal body. So then, death is at work in us, but life is at work in you' (2 Cor 4:11–12)

§

From time to time, when the existential pain has been acute, I have had to run away, find a place to hide, and lay down and 'die'.

When I was excommunicated by YWAM from Dilaram I experienced a terrible sense of rejection. People denounced me publicly, forbade anyone I knew to have anything to do with me, and threatened anyone who gave me shelter with immediate excommunication.

I felt this rejection as a physical pain in the centre of my chest — as if I was literally heart broken. Any time I bumped into a YWAMer I would shake with fear. So I packed my bags, went home, and stayed home — out of sight. During that time I used to drive into my driveway, park the car, run upstairs, close the door, pull the curtains and hide from people who might come by and knock at the door. On a number of occasions I actually withdrew into my bedroom, lay down on my bed, curled up into a foetal position, hugged myself for comfort, and waited to die. And, on one such occasion, I felt such despair that I contemplated killing myself. I don't know whether I would have really been able to kill myself or not, but the fact that I was thinking about it made me realise that I was in big trouble — I had internalised the rejection to such a degree that now I was even rejecting myself.

I needed help, but didn't know where to find it. At this stage, I was a *persona non grata*. Most of the Christians I knew had either turned their back on me or had been treated just like me, and others I talked to didn't understand. In desperation, I turned to God for help. I used to find solace in God quite easily, but now it was quite difficult because the very 'word of God' had been used to condemn me, and I felt profoundly alienated from God by God's people.

As it turned out, my salvation was in the fact that my experience of the *love of God* was deeper than my experience of *alienation from God*. Through Christ, I was able to come to God and experience his magical, mystical, amazing love for me. 'Come to me' Christ said 'and I will offer you a place of rest, an oasis to restore your soul for the journey.' 'Abide in me' he said 'and I'll abide with you. Together we'll be friends and you can ask of me whatever you like and I'll do it for you.'[194]

So I came to him as a leper — my body dripping with sores, my soul hungry for belonging — and I knelt before him; and Christ reached out to me and touched me, enfolded me in his arms, embraced me in his love, and healed my broken heart. Fragrant, unconditional, limitless love running down, like thick olive oil, into the recesses of my wounded soul. Refreshing, renewing, reforming, redeeming grace, filling the void inside with the joy of being loved — and being able to love again.

As a result, I have been able to develop the capacity to reconnect with people who have hurt me. Indeed, I cannot think of one person I have had a conflict with, whom I have not deliberately gone out of my way to try to reconcile with. Even in YWAM.

Last year, some thirty years after the event, I was able to visit the YWAM base in Europe where I had been excommunicated. I was received very warmly by the current European Director and his wife, who not only apologised to me for the way I had been treated, but promised me that they would do their best to make sure in future that dissidents in YWAM would not be treated like I was. Every now and again I get an invitation to teach YWAMers in my own home town on how to work with marginalised and disadvantaged people. And there is nothing that I enjoy more than being able to walk back into an organisation that very nearly totally destroyed me and help them consider how they can work with 'the poor and needy'.

In an emergency, when the pain is acute, all of us — like Paul, — need to be able to give ourselves permission to run and hide for weeks, months, even years; to develop the capacity to die inside, yet stay alive, rising anew to the next challenge; and — when we are ready — try again to restore broken relationships in the spirit of the risen Christ.

§

However, it is my contention, that we will only be able to deal with the *acute* pain we face in a crisis well, if we learn to deal with the *chronic* pain we face constantly.

A little while ago Ange, and I decided to see how our friends were doing twenty years after we'd started our own faith-based community revolution. Ange and I had been hard at it, and were feeling frazzled from the relentless stress involved in doing our bit for our do-it-yourself contemporary church reformation. We also thought it might cheer us up to catch up with some of our comrades. Our friends were now dispersed all over the planet, so we had to save up to buy 'round-the-world' tickets to visit them. We eventually got the money together for the tickets, and took off for our '*chai*-and-chat' tour of India, Nepal, Australia, New Zealand, Canada, the US and the UK.

It was just what the doctor ordered for us. It was a real 'pick-me-up' tonic, to have the chance just to sit and talk over a cuppa with people that we had known in our youth and who, as middle-aged men and women, were struggling with the same issues in their lives as we were. We noted that they — like us — were battling to maintain their commitment to integrity, family and community, against immense external pressures, and constant internal temptations, to chuck it all in. All of them bore the scars that came from battling to maintain their commitment. We also noticed that they — like us — were continuing to be committed to altruistic causes, but with less energy and less enthusiasm as more time went by. While most of them were still involved in causes, such as human rights, social justice and community development, most were moving away from direct personal participation, towards indirect professional association. Few of us were engaged as passionately in the work for change as we had been.

For Ange and me, the question was not about why so many of us were beginning to falter — we knew full well why. Years ago I had written a book called *Can You Hear The Heartbeat?*, and my friends suggested that it was about time that I wrote a sequel entitled *Can't You See The Heartbreak?* We had chosen to care, and we were crushed by the unbearable weight of despair that came with hoping and praying and working for so much, but accomplishing so little. The question for Ange and I was not *why* so many of us were faltering, but *how* some of us were managing to keep the faith, and continue to 'fight the good fight'. To answer that question, we paid particularly close attention to the conversations we had with a few of our friends who were slogging away, as fervently as ever, at the task of transformation. And, in listening to them talk about their lives, Ange and I were able to distinguish three classical trinitarian characteristics which — combined together — seemed to contribute to their capacity to sustain the radical quality of their resolve, year in, year out (see Table 5).

The *first* characteristic we were able to distinguish, that seemed to give our friends a radical edge, *was their appreciation of the Love of God*. It was their ongoing, intimate, existential experience of the amazing, magical, mystical love at the heart of the universe, that inspired hope in the possibility of redemption, in spite of disappointments, and infused their wounded, weary hearts with a renewed capacity to love.

The *second* characteristic *was their commitment to the Call of Christ*. For them, vocation was not a call 'to be someone else', like someone more successful or more famous. For them, vocation was a call 'to become themselves' — not a person *like* others, but a person *for* others — as faithfully as they could; and to be renewed in the joy of being who they knew they really were, in spite of the names other people might call them.

The *third* characteristic *was their accountability in the Spirit of Truth*. None of them were saints. They all had problems, which left unresolved would be inimical to their progress. But, instead of denying their contradictions, they dealt with them — by welcoming feedback from people who knew their problems, and were committed to resolution.

An Ongoing Program for Chronic Pain	
Part One	An Ongoing Appreciation Of The Love Of God
Part Two	An Ongoing Commitment To The Call Of Christ
Part Three	An Ongoing Accountability In The Spirit Of Truth

Table 5: An Ongoing Program for Chronic Pain

Ange and I are very intentional about maintaining this approach, as a way of dealing with our chronic existential pain, so that it does not ever completely cripple us.

We seek to maintain our ongoing encounter of the Love of God. We live in the tension between two mutually exclusive polarities of experience simultaneously. On the one hand, we feel that in choosing to care we continually get wounded. But, on the other hand, we feel that by bringing our selves to God, and placing our selves in his hands, we have no wounds so great that we cannot hope for healing. We daily die the death of a thousand cuts. And daily seek — and find — solace in his love.

We seek to maintain our ongoing commitment to the Call of Christ. We are tempted to want to try to live our lives like our heroes. I would like to be Mahatma Gandhi, and Ange would like to be Mother Theresa. However, we constantly come back to Christ's call to be our true selves, and not someone else — no matter how good or kind.

We seek to maintain our ongoing accountability in the Spirit of Truth. We really try to be accountable to one another 'in spirit and in truth'. Each morning Ange and I meet to monitor how we are going. Recently I was depressed, and Ange asked me straight to my face whether I had died without her knowing it — because, she said, living with me was like 'living with a dead man'. That was enough to make me realize I had to get help to get myself together. So I sought professional help and sorted myself out. Yet again.

If we are going to cope with the chronic pain involved in working for change, then all of us need to adapt a program like this to our own needs — and adopt it as our own!

§

Michael Schluter — director of the Jubilee Centre, a UK think tank — asked himself what the 'biggest idea' was that he had found in the Bible. He says,

> The answer was found to be as simple as it was profound. After replying to a slightly different question from a lawyer, Jesus went on to address directly the question I was asking:
>
> 'Teacher, which is the greatest commandment in the Law?' Jesus replied: 'Love the Lord your God with all your heart and with all your soul and with all your mind.' This is the first and greatest commandment. And the second is like it: 'Love your neighbour as yourself.' All the Law and the Prophets hang on these two commandments' (Mt 22:36–40).
>
> Love, of course, is not the language of finance or economics: it is the language of relationships. God measures a society, by the quality of its relationships. Such a finding is hardly surprising.[195]

The religion of the Bible is a relational religion. As John Zizioulas has observed, 'The chief lesson is that if God is essentially relational, then all being shares in relation: there is, that is to say, a relational content built into the nature of being. To be is to exist in relation to other beings.'[196]

Schluter writes:

> The relational approach can be used to critique legislation and the structures and working practices of organisations. It offers an alternative ethos for sectors of public policy, for example 'relational justice' for the criminal justice system and 'relational healthcare' for the NHS. In these and other ways the relational approach, informed by biblical principles, can provide a reform agenda for public life...For those who are convinced that it is possible to derive a biblically based agenda for political, economic and social reform using the relational approach...it is essential not just to analyse what is wrong in society but also to try and change it. The day of the think tanks is passing away; it is no longer sufficient simply to promote ideas at an intellectual level. Policy is made increasingly after practical experiment, pilot schemes and regional initiatives.[197]

Just like the service at St Andrew's. If a relational approach is accepted as a strategy for political and personal engagement, Schluter states that

> we can expect widespread reform initiatives at national, regional and local levels based on relational thinking. Those in national and local politics, in business and financial services, in the professions and in caring roles will work to a fresh agenda.[198]

Whether a relational approach has a long-term impact on society will depend, Schluter says, 'on whether it stays in touch with its biblical roots. Divorced from biblical teaching, it will lack the cutting edge derived from the wisdom in Scripture.' If constantly renewed 'with the insights of biblical reflection', Schluter writes, the radical relational approach advocated in Scripture 'may challenge successfully the dominant ideologies of global capitalism and market socialism.'[199]

§

We need to be continually renewed in the spirit of community that we have been introduced to through the Trinity, so that each step we take in community development will be inspired by the radical spirituality of the divine society to which we aspire.

No one has portrayed that spirit better in the Bible than Jesus in his Sermon on the Mount, and no one has summarised the Sermon on the Mount better than Paul, so let us conclude our reflections with the words we have often referred to throughout this book:

> Let love be genuine; hate what is evil, hold fast to what is good; love one another with mutual affection; outdo one another in showing honour. Do not lag in zeal, be ardent in spirit, serve the Lord. Rejoice in hope, be patient in suffering, persevere in prayer. Contribute to the needs of the saints; extend hospitality to strangers.
> Bless those who persecute you; bless and do not curse them. Rejoice with those who rejoice; weep with those who weep. Live in harmony with one another; do not be haughty, but associate with the lowly; do not claim to be wiser than you are. Do not repay anyone evil for evil, but take thought for what is noble in the sight of all. If it is possible, so far as it depends on you, live peaceably with all…If your enemies are hungry, feed them; if they are thirsty, give them something to drink…Do not be overcome by evil, but overcome evil with good. (Rom 12:9–18, 20–21)

CAUTION: 'THOSE WHO LOVE COMMUNITY DESTROY COMMUNITY; ONLY THOSE WHO LOVE PEOPLE CREATE COMMUNITY'

It is all too easy for us to destroy the very thing we seek to create. So, we would be well advised to listen carefully to what those who have gone before us have to say about how we need to approach the hazardous process of community development.

The following are a series of quotations from experienced community animators on crucial aspects of community development that I would encourage you to reflect on.

On creating a safe space

A true community is a *safe space* where — Henri Nouwen reminds us — our tendency towards hostility needs to be transformed into the capacity to extend real hospitality:

> We can say that during the last years strangers have become more and more subject to hostility than to hospitality... In a world so pervaded with competition, even those who are very close to each other...can become infected by hostility when they experience each other as a threat to their safety... We are called to move (from hostility to) hospitality. The German word of hospitality is *'Gastfreundschaft'*, which means friendship for the guest. The Dutch word for hospitality, *'gastvrijheid'*, means the freedom of the guest. [I]t shows hospitality wants to offer friendship without binding the guest, freedom without leaving [the guest] alone. Hospitality, therefore, means primarily the creation of a free space where the stranger can enter and become a friend instead of an enemy. Hospitality is not to change people, but to offer them space where change can take place. It is not to bring men and women over to our side, but to offer freedom not disturbed by dividing lines. It is not to lead our neighbour into a corner where there are no alternatives left, but to open a wide spectrum of options for choice and commitment. It is

> not an educated intimidation with good books, good stories
> and good work, but the liberation of fearful hearts... The
> paradox of hospitality is that it wants to create emptiness,
> not a fearful emptiness, but a friendly emptiness, where
> strangers can enter and discover themselves as created free
> — free to sing their own songs, speak their own languages,
> dance their own dances; free also to leave and follow their
> own vocations. Hospitality is not a subtle invitation to adopt
> the life style of the host, but the gift of a chance for the guest
> to find (their) own.[200]

Hostility destroys community. Hospitality restores community. A divine society, incarnating the trinity in community, is the creation of a free, friendly, safe space.

On extending acceptance

A true community is *as a place where people are accepted as part of a group*. If people are forgotten, rejected, or ignored, they don't feel part of a group. It is only if people are remembered, acknowledged and recognised as people that they feel part of a group. According to Jean Vanier, the founder and leader of L'Arche, community is all about the constant practice of unconditional acceptance over and above the erratic byplay of petty sympathies and antipathies.

> The two great dangers of community are 'friends' and
> 'enemies'. People very quickly get together with those who
> are like themselves; we all like to be with someone who
> shares our ways of looking at life. Human friendships can
> very quickly become a club of mediocrities, enclosed in
> mutual flattery. Friendship is then no longer a spur to grow,
> to go further, to be of greater service to our brothers and
> sisters. Friendship then becomes a barrier between ourselves
> and others. There are always people with whom we don't
> agree, who block us, who contradict us. We seem incapable
> of expressing ourselves or even of living peacefully, when
> we are with them. Others ask too much of us; we cannot

> respond to their incessant demands and we have to push them away. These are the 'enemies'. They endanger us, and, even if we dare not admit it, we hate them. Certainly, this is not deliberate. But even so, we wish these people didn't exist! These affinities and aversions between different personalities are natural. They come from an emotional immaturity and from many elements from our childhood over which we have no control. It would be foolish to deny them. But if we let ourselves be guided by our emotional reactions, cliques will form....It will no longer be a community, a place of communion, but a collection of people more or less...cut off one from another. When you go into some communities, you can quickly sense tensions...People don't look each other in the face. They pass each other in the corridors like ships in the night. A community is only a community when most of the members have consciously decided to break these barriers and come out of their 'friendship(s)' to [reach] out to their 'enemies'.[201]

Both affinities and aversions create cliques. Only a spirit of real acceptance can create a divine society.

On expressing respect

A true community *a place where there is respect for the unity and the diversity of people in a group*. If there is no respect for unity, there is no group. However, if there is no respect for diversity, there is no place for various people in a given group. According to community facilitator, M Scott Peck, community is all about the constant practice of dedicated inclusivity over against dismissive exclusivity.

> Community is inclusive. The great enemy of community is exclusivity. Groups that exclude others because they are poor or doubters or sinners or of some different race or nationality are not communities: they are cliques — actually defensive bastions against community.
> Inclusiveness is not an absolute (But) true communities, on

the other hand, if they want to remain such, are always reaching to extend themselves. Communities do not ask 'How can we justify taking this person in?' Instead the question is: 'Is it at all justifiable to keep this person out?' In relation to other groupings communities are always relatively inclusive. (T)he inclusiveness of any community extends along all it's parameters. There is an 'allness' to community. It is not merely a matter of including different sexes, races, and creeds. It is also inclusive of the full range of human emotions. Tears are as welcome as laughter, fear as well as faith. And different styles: hawks and doves, straights and gays, the talkative and the silent. All human differences are included. Exclusivity, the great enemy to community, appears in two forms: excluding the other and excluding yourself. If you conclude under your breath, 'Well, this group just isn't for me, I'm just going to go.' it would be as destructive to community as it would be to a marriage. Community, like marriage, requires that we hang in there when the going gets a little rough. It requires a certain degree of commitment. If we do hang in there, we usually find after a while that 'the rough places are made plain'. A friend correctly defined community as 'a group that has learned to transcend its differences'. 'Transcend' does not mean 'obliterate'. It literally means 'to climb over'. The achievement of community can be compared to the reaching of a mountaintop'.[202]

Exclusive unity creates conformity, and exclusive diversity creates incompatibility. Only a spirit of unity and diversity that is inclusive can create a divine society.

On exercising care

A true community is *a place where there is responsibility for the welfare of each person in the group*. If the group is to fulfil its function, it cannot exist as an end in itself. The group exists as a means to the end of helping people to grow as people. According to Jean Vanier, community is all about the constant practice of conscious responsibility for empowering people — enabling them to realise their potential.

> In community people care for each other, and not just for the community in the abstract as an institution or as an ideal way of life. It is people that matter; to care for the people that are there, just as they are. And it is not just caring in a passing way but in a permanent way. So many people enter groups in order to develop a certain form of spirituality, or to acquire knowledge about humanity. But that is not community. (I)t becomes community only when people start truly caring for each other's growth. Esther de Waal writing about the Rule of St Benedict, (guidelines for the religious living together in community), says: 'It is noticeable how the abbot and the cellerer are concerned about the (people), caring for each singly in all their uniqueness, rather than with the community *en bloc*, that ideal which seems to haunt so much contemporary ideology. The common life never becomes a piece of abstract idealisation or idealism. St Benedict would probably have appreciated Dietrich Bonhoeffer's aphorism: 'Those who love community, destroy community, those who love people build community.' Some communities — which are more sects — tend to suppress the individual…in the interest of a greater unity. They tend to stop people from thinking…Everyone must think alike…Unity here is based on fear — the fear of being yourself. Community must never take precedence over people. It is for people and for their growth. In fact it's beauty…come(s) from the radiance of each person (as they grow) in their truth, (and their) love.[203]

Individual concern creates individuality, and collective concern creates collectivity. Only a spirit of real care for people as persons can create a divine society.

On enabling participation

A true community is *a place where there is participation — by every person in the group — in the decisions of the group*. People do not expect to make every decision that affects them. However, if they are part of a group, people expect to play a part in every decision the group makes that affects them. According to John Cobb, community is all about the constant practice of conscientious participation by every member of a group in the decisions that affect their lives.

> To have a communal character...does not entail intimacy among all the participants. It does entail that membership in the society contributes to self-identification (and self-development). To illustrate, for the alienated youth in large cities, those cities remain the societies of which they are members, but they do not constitute, for them, communities. A society should not be called a community unless there is extensive participation by it's members in the decisions by which it's life is governed. By (this) definition there can be a totalitarian society but there can be no totalitarian community.
> (C)ommunity is a matter of...the extent to which (a society) participate(s) in its governance.[204]

M Scott Peck writes:

> We are so unfamiliar with genuine community that we have never developed an adequate vocabulary for the politics ... When we ponder on how individual differences can be accommodated, perhaps the first mechanism we turn to (probably because it is the most childlike) is that of the strong individual leader. Differences, like those of squabbling siblings, we instinctively think can be resolved by a mommy or daddy — a benevolent dictator, or so we hope. But community, encouraging individuality as it does, can never be totalitarian. So we jump to a somewhat less primitive way of resolving individual differences which we call democracy.

> We take a vote, and the majority determines which differences prevail. Majority rules. Yet that process excludes the aspirations of the minority.
> How do we transcend differences in such a way as to include a minority? It seems like a conundrum. How do you go beyond democracy? In the genuine communities of which I have been a member, a thousand or more group decisions have been made, and I have never yet witnessed a vote. I do not mean to imply that we...should discard democratic machinery, any more than we should abolish organization. But I do mean to imply that a community, in transcending individual differences, routinely goes beyond even democracy. In the vocabulary of this transcendence we thus far have only one word: 'consensus'. Decisions in genuine community are arrived at through consensus, in a process that is not unlike a community of jurors, for whom consensual decision making is mandated.[205]

Autocracy creates a satisfied minority at odds with a dissatisfied majority. Democracy creates a satisfied majority at odds with a dissatisfied minority. Only a spirit of real consensus can create a divine society that fulfils the aspirations of its constituents.

On embodying justice

Last but not least, *a true community is a place where there is support for processes that do justice to the disadvantaged* — not only those inside, but also those outside the group. People do not expect all their needs to be met, but they do expect a group that is concerned for people, to do all it can to help them meet their basic unmet needs. According to Amatai Etzioni, community is all about the constant practice of consistent support for processes that do justice to the most disadvantaged, whether they are part of the group or not.

> A communitarian position on social justice (for all groups) includes the following elements:

First, people have a moral responsibility to help themselves as best as they can. At first it may seem heartless to ask...but it is respectful of human dignity to encourage people to control their fate the best they can...People should not be exempt from responsibility for themselves.

The second line of responsibility lies with those closest to the person, including kin, neighbours, and other community members. They are next in line because they know best what the genuine needs are...and are able to tailor the help to what is required.(W)hen the government provides meals on wheels, everybody either eats the same meals or must choose from a limited menu. But when neighbours take turns bringing food to a...needy person, they can take into account personal tastes...

For the same reason, as a rule, every community ought to be expected to do the best it can to look after it's own...Society, as a community of communities, should encourage the... expectation that attending to welfare is the responsibility of the local community. We follow this rule already when there is a fire. The local fire company is the first one to be called in; only if it cannot handle the blaze are companies from other communities mobilized.

Last but not least, societies, which are nothing but communities of communities, must help those communities whose ability to help their members is severely limited. Charity ought to begin at home, but not end at home. Each community must be expected to reach out to members of other communities that are less well endowed and hence less well able to deal with their own problems. Social justice is an inter-community issue.[206]

Injustice anywhere is injustice everywhere. A divine society will be committed to practicing justice — in ever expanding circles of concern — to the ends of the earth.

Towards a global ethic

In 1993, Dr. Hans Kung, the famous Catholic theologian, in cooperation with the trustees and staff of the Council for a Parliament of the World's Religions, drafted a declaration that unpacked the implications of these covenants for an ethic to bless the peoples of the earth. At the Parliament, an assembly of religious leaders gave its formal assent to the document called *Declaration Toward a Global Ethic*. The document is a powerful statement of the common ground shared by the world's spiritual traditions, and has emerged as a significant building block in the continuing process of creating global covenantal understanding and consensus:

> The world is in agony. The agony is so pervasive and urgent that we are compelled to name its manifestations so that the depth of this pain may be made clear.
>
> Peace eludes us — the planet is being destroyed — neighbors live in fear — women and men are estranged from each other — children die!
>
> This is abhorrent.
>
> We condemn the abuses of Earth's ecosystems.
>
> We condemn the poverty that stifles life's potential; the hunger that weakens the human body, the economic disparities that threaten so many families with ruin.
>
> We condemn the social disarray of the nations; the disregard for justice which pushes citizens to the margin; the anarchy overtaking our communities; and the insane death of children from violence. In particular we condemn aggression and hatred in the name of religion.
>
> But this agony need not be.

It need not be because the basis for an ethic already exists. This ethic offers the possibility of a better individual and global order, and leads individuals away from despair and societies away from chaos.

We are women and men who have embraced the precepts and practices of the world's religions:

We affirm that a common set of core values is found in the teachings of the religions, and that these form the basis of a global ethic.

We affirm that this truth is already known, but yet to be lived in heart and action.

We affirm that there is an irrevocable, unconditional norm for all areas of life, for families and communities, for races, nations, and religions. There already exist ancient guidelines for human behaviour which are found in the teachings of the religions of the world and which are the condition for a sustainable world order.

We declare:

We are interdependent. Each of us depends on the well-being of the whole, and so we have respect for the community of living beings, for people, animals, and plants, and for the preservation of Earth, the air, water and soil.

We take individual responsibility for all we do. All our decisions, actions, and failures to act have consequences.

We must treat others as we wish others to treat us. We make a commitment to respect life and dignity, individuality and diversity, so that every person is treated humanely, without exception. We must have patience and acceptance. We must be able to forgive, learning from the past but never allowing ourselves to be enslaved by memories of hate. Opening our hearts to one another, we must sink our narrow differences for the cause of the world community, practicing a culture of [207] solidarity and relatedness.

We consider humankind our family. We must strive to be kind and generous. We must not live for ourselves alone, but should also serve others, never forgetting the children, the aged, the poor, the suffering, the disabled, the refugees, and the lonely. No person should ever be considered or treated as a second-class citizen, or be exploited in any way whatsoever. There should be equal partnership between men and women. We must not commit any kind of sexual immorality. We must put behind us all forms of domination or abuse.

We commit ourselves to a culture of non-violence, respect, justice, and peace. We shall not oppress, injure, torture, or kill other human beings, forsaking violence as a means of settling differences.

We must strive for a just social and economic order, in which everyone has an equal chance to reach full potential as a human being. We must speak and act truthfully and with compassion, dealing fairly with all, and avoiding prejudice and hatred. We must not steal. We must move beyond the dominance of greed for power, prestige, money, and consumption to make a just and peaceful world.

Earth cannot be changed for the better unless the consciousness of individuals is changed first. We pledge to increase our awareness by disciplining our minds, by meditation, by prayer, or by positive thinking. Without risk and a readiness to sacrifice there can be no fundamental change in our situation. Therefore we commit ourselves to this global ethic, to understanding one another, and to socially beneficial, peace-fostering, and nature-friendly ways of life.

We invite all people, whether religious or not, to do the same.

REFERENCES

1 C. Bell & H. Newby, *Community Studies* (London: Allen & Unwin, 1971), p. 2.
2 R. Williams, *Keywords: A Vocabulary of Culture and Society* (London: Fontana, 1976), p. 66.
3 D. Clark, *Basic Communities* (London: SPCK, 1975), pp. 4–5.
4 H. Mackay, *Turning Point*, (Sydney: Macmillan, 1999), p. 256.
5 R. Putnam, *Bowling Alone* (New York: Simon & Schuster, 2001), p. 327.
6 R. Putnam, p. 332.
7 R. Putnam, pp. 136–8.
8 R. Putnam, pp. 118–121.
9 R. Putnam, p. 319.
10 R. Putnam, p. 147.
11 R. Putnam, pp. 308–309, 310.
12 P. Westoby, *Soulful Community Development* (Woollongabba: Community Praxis Co-op Ltd, 2001), vol. 1, p. 8.
13 P. Westoby, *Training And Soul* (Woollongabba: Community Praxis Co-op Ltd, 2002), vol. 2, p. 9.
14 P. Westoby, pp. 39–40.
15 C. Baxter Kruger, *The Great Dance* (Jackson, MS: Perichoresis Press, 2002).
16 I. Kant, *Der Streit der Fakultaten* (Berlin: 1917) vol. 8, pp. 38–9.
17 L. Boff, *Trinity And Society* (London: Burns & Oates, 1988), pp. 15–16, 119.
18 http://www.stjohnscamberwell.org.au/Sermons/ExplanationofTheTrinityIcon.htm
19 B. McEntee, *Rublev's Icon Of The Trinity*, http://www.materdei.ie/logos/E4_TLR.htm
20 J. Macmurray, *The Self As Agent* (London: Faber and Faber, 1957), pp. 84–85, 86–89.
21 J. Macmurray, *Reason and Emotion* (London: Faber and Faber, 1935), p. 22.
22 C. Baxter Kruger, *The Great Dance* (Jackson, MS: Perichoresis Press, 2002), p. 19.

23 J. Macmurray, *Persons In Relation* (London: Faber and Faber, 1961), pp. 184–185.

24 C. Baxter Kruger, *The Great Dance* (Jackson, MS: Perichoresis Press, 2002), p. 19.

25 B. McEntee, *Rublev's Icon Of The Trinity*, http://www.materdei.ie/logos/E4_TLR.htm

26 M. Buber, *To Hallow This Life* (CT: Greenwood Press, 1966).

27 A. Etzioni, *Next: The Road to the Good Society* (New York: Basic Books, 2001), pp. 5–6.

28 A. Kelly & S. Sewell, *With Head Heart And Hand* (Brisbane: Boolarong, 1989), p, 62.

29 R. Jenson, 'The Father, He…', in A. Kimel (ed.), *Speaking The Christian God* (Grand Rapids, MI: Eerdmans, 1992), p. 104.

30 P. Fiddes, *Participating In God* (London: Darton, Longman and Todd, 2000), pp. 89–91.

31 L. Boff, *Trinity And Society* (Maryknoll, NY: Orbis Books, 1988), p. 236.

32 L. Boff, p. 141.

33 P. Fiddes, *Participating In God*, (London: Darton, Longman and Todd, 2000), p. 66.

34 J. Moltmann, quoted by M Volf, *After Our Own Likeness* (Grand Rapids, MI: Eerdmans, 1998), p. 210.

35 P. Fiddes, *Participating In God* (London: Darton, Longman and Todd, 2000), p. 78.

36 C. Baxter Kruger, *The Great Dance* (Jackson, MS: Perichoresis Press, 2002), pp. 20, 78, 79.

37 P. Fiddes, *Participating In God* (London: Darton, Longman and Todd, 2000), p. 91.

38 Adapted from J. Macquarie, *Principles Of Christian Theology* (London, SCM Press, 1977), pp. 200-2.

39 Adapted from S. McFague, *The Body Of God* (London: SCM Press, 1993), pp. 161–2.

40 C. Schwarz, *The Threefold Art Of Experiencing God* (Carol Stream: ChurchSmart Resources, 1999), pp 6–19.

41 Composite based on a figure in C. Wright, *Living As The People Of God* (Leicester: IVP, 1983), p. 19. Image by L. Whalen in T. Hampson,

Tales of the Heart, (New York: Friendship Press, 1991), p. 30.

42 C. Birch, *On Purpose* (Kensington: New South Wales University Press, 1990), p. 90.
43 C. Wright, *Living As The People Of God* (Leicester: IVP, 1983), p. 19.
44 M. Riddell, *Godzone* (Oxford: Lion, 1992), p. 30.
45 M. Riddell, pp. 23–4.
46 J. Olthuis, *The Beautiful Risk* (Grand Rapids, MI: Zondervan, 2001).
47 C. Baxter Kruger, *The Great Dance* (Jackson, MS: Perichoresis Press, 2002, pp. 79, 60–61, 82.
48 D. Benner, *Surrender to Love* (Downers Grove: IVP, 2003), pp. 61–63, 79.
49 W. Muller, *Legacy Of The Heart* (New York: Simon & Schuster, 1992), p. 27. See Isaiah 40:31.
50 D. Benner, *Surrender to Love* (Downers Grove: IVP, 2003), pp. 84–5.
51 W. Muller, *Legacy Of The Heart* (New York: Simon & Schuster, 1992), p. 27.
52 D. Benner, *Surrender to Love* (Downers Grove: IVP, 2003), pp. 93–4.
53 A.N. Whitehead, *Process and Reality* (New York: Macmillan, 1929), pp. 69ff.
54 P. Fiddes, *Participating In God* (London: Darton, Longman and Todd, 2000), p. 145.
55 M. Jegen and B. Manno, *The Earth Is The Lord's* (New York: Paulist Press, 1978), p. 24.
56 F. Schaeffer, *Genesis In Space And Time* (London: Hodder and Stoughton, 1972), pp. 33–34.
57 W. Berry, *Another Turn of The Crank* (Washington: Counterpoint, 1995), pp. 74, 77.
58 W. Berry, p. 73.
59 W. Berry, *Life Is A Miracle* (Washington: Counterpoint, 2001), pp. 41, 137–8.
60 W. Berry, *Another Turn of The Crank* (Washington: Counterpoint, 1995), p. 73.
61 W. Berry, *In the Presence Of Fear* (Great Barrington: Orion Society, 2001), p. 30.
62 W. Berry, p. 31.
63 H. H. Farmer, *The World And God* (London: Nisbet, 1935), p. 24.

64 P. Fiddes, *Participating In God* (London: Darton, Longman and Todd, 2000), p. 131.
65 J. P. Satre, 'Existentialism Is A Humanism', in W. Kaufmann, *Existentialism from Dostoevsky to Sartre* (Cleveland, OH: Meridian Books, 1946), p. 33.
66 W. Berry, *Another Turn of The Crank* (Washington: Counterpoint, 1995), p. 76.
67 W. Berry, p. 75.
68 D. Bonhoeffer, cited by P. Tyson, *Tower of Babel* (Brisbane: unpublished manuscript, 2004), p. 1.
69 P. Palmer, pp. 7–8.
70 N. Noddings, *Caring* (Berkeley: University of California Press, 1986), p. 86.
71 C. Hamilton, *Growth Fetish* (Crows Nest: Allen & Unwin, 2003), p. 174.
72 C. Hamilton, pp. 174–188.
73 P. Tyson, *Tower of Babel* (Brisbane: unpublished manuscript, 2004), pp. 1–2.
74 P. Tyson, p. 1.
75 J. Sacks, *The Politics of Hope* (New York: Random House, 2000), p. 55.
76 J. Sacks, pp. 55ff.
77 J. Sacks, pp. 55-65.
78 J. Sacks, pp. 55–65.
79 Daniel Elazar and Stuart Cohen, *The Jewish Polity* (Bloomington: Indiana University Press, 1984), p. 4.
80 Daniel Elazar and Stuart Cohen, p. 4.
81 Daniel Elazar, *People and Polity* (Detroit: Wayne State University Press, 1989), p. 19.
82 Hugh Davies, *Leadership in Servants* (Manila: unpublished manuscript, 2007), p. 27.
83 J. Sacks, *The Politics of Hope* (New York: Random House, 2000), pp. 55–65.
84 H. Kung, *Christianity* (London, SCM, 1995), p. 34.
85 H Kung, p. 35.
86 C. Baxter Kruger, *The Great Dance* (Jackson, MS: Perichoresis Press,

2002), pp. 56–7.
87 Excerpt from D. Andrews, *Christi-Anarchy* (Oxford: Lion, 1999), pp. 108–113.
88 C. Baxter Kruger, *The Great Dance* (Jackson, MS: Perichoresis Press, 2002), p. 24.
89 W. Popkes, *Christus Traditus* (Zurich: Zwingliverlag, 1967), p. 286.
90 J. Moltmann, *The Way Of Christ* (London: SCM, 1990), p. 176.
91 J. Moltmann, p. 173.
92 T. McAlpine, *Facing The Powers* (Monrovia, CA: MARC, 1991), p. 15.
93 T. McAlpine, p. 12.
94 Unpublished lesson outline, Brisbane State High School, p. 1.
95 H. Berkof, *Christ and the Powers* (Scottdale, PA: Herald, 1962), pp. 30ff.
96 W. Wink, *Engaging The Powers* (Minneapolis: Fortress, 1992), pp. 139–140.
97 W. Wink, pp. 139–140.
98 G. Sharp, *Power and Struggle* (Boston: Porter Sargent, 1973), pp. 11–12, 18–24.
99 S. Kennedy, *The Best Of G.A. Studdert Kennedy* (London: Hodder and Stoughton, 1963), p. 84.
100 T. Boomershine, *Story Journey* (Nashville: Abingdon, 1988), p. 171.
101 E. Wiesel, *Night* (New York: Hill and Wang, 1960), p. 70ff.
102 E. Wiesel, p. 1.
103 G. Preston, 'Just when did Australia's Christians decide that abortion is oaky after all?', in Terry Gatfield, *Contemporary Christian Issues* (Brisbane: Heritage, 1998), p. 14.
104 D. Andrews, *Building A Better World* (Sutherland: Albatross), p. 262.
105 W. Deane, *Some Signposts From Daguragu: The Inaugural Lingiari Lecture* (Canberra: Council for Aboriginal Reconciliation, 1996), p. 26.
106 P. Dodson, *The Path To Reconciliation* (Canberra: Commonwealth of Australia, 1997), p. 29.
107 *Back Door Letter on East Timor*, http://members.canb.auug.org.au/~wildwood/kopassus.htm updated Feb. 13, 2002.
108 W. Barclay, p. 109.
109 D. Andrews, 'The Mad Monk', *Target*, No.1, 2000, p. 19.
110 Adapted from D. Andrews, 'The Mad Monk', *Target*, No.1, 2000, p. 19.
111 F. Beuchner, *The Magnificent Defeat* (San Francisco: Harper Collins,

1966), p. 65.
112. G. Webbe, *The Night and Nothing* (New York: Seabury Press, 1964), p. 109.
113. M. S. Peck, *The People Of The Lie* (New York: Simon & Schuster, 1983), p. 269.
114. W. Barclay, *Crucified and Crowned*, (SCM, 1961), pp. 134, 130, 129.
115. M. Gandhi, *An Autobiography* (Ahmedabad: The Navjivan Press, 1927), pp. 90–92.
116. M. Gandhi, *An Autobiography* (Ahmedabad: The Navjivan Press, 1927), pp. 92.
117. Matthew 6:10.
118. C. Christos, *Letters From A Prisoner Of Conscience* (London: Lutterworth Press, 1978), pp. 15–16.
119. W. Barclay, *Crucified and Crowned* (SCM, 1961), p. 95.
120. Composite based on a drawing by T. Jordon, Dayspring House Of Freedom, Brisbane.
121. A. Armstrong, quoted by P. Fiddes, *Participating In God* (London: Darton, Longman and Todd, 2000), p. 255.
122. P. Fiddes, p. 255.
123. W. Muller, *Legacy Of The Heart* (New York: Simon & Schuster, 1992), p. 47.
124. A. Johnson, *The Vitality of the Individual in the Thought of Ancient Israel* (Cardiff: University of Wales Press, 1964), p. 30–32.
125. P. Fiddes, *Participating In God* (London: Darton, Longman and Todd, 2000), p. 257.
126. J. Moltmann, *The Church In The Power Of The Spirit* (London, SCM, 1977), pp. 301, 302.
127. C. Baxter Kruger, *The Great Dance* (Jackson, MS: Perichoresis Press, 2002), p. 28.
128. C. Baxter Kruger, pp. 89–91.
129. J. Moltmann, *The Church In The Power Of The Spirit* (London: SCM, 1977), p. 295.
130. P. Palmer, *Let Your Life Speak* (San Francisco: Jossey-Bass, 2000), pp. 49, 32–34, 16.
131. J. V. Taylor, *The Go-Between God* (London: SCM Press, 1972), pp. 11–12.

132 J. V. Taylor, pp. 6, 8, 15–18, 20.
133 J. V. Taylor, p. 18.
134 J. V. Taylor, pp. 18, 21–22, 29, 126–7.
135 J. V. Taylor, p. 243.
136 G. Hillery, 'Definitions of Community: Areas of Agreement', *Rural Sociology*, vol. 20, no. 2, 1955, p. 118.
137 D. Clark, *Basic Communities* (London: SPCK, 1975), pp. 4–5.
138 M.S. Peck, *The Different Drum* (London: Rider and Company, 1988), p. 59.
139 F. Toennies, *Community And Society* (New York: Harper, 1957), pp. 12–29.
140 R. Putnam, quoted by M. Jonas, 'The Downside of Diversity', *The Boston Globe*, August 5 2007, viewed 10/11/07, http://www.boston.com/news/globe/ideas/articles/2007/08/05/the_downside_of_diversity/
141 P. Palmer, *The Company Of Strangers* (New York: Crossroad, 1985), pp. 56, 57.
142 P. Palmer, p. 57.
143 P. Palmer, p. 58.
144 P. Palmer, p. 58.
145 F. Peavey, 'Strategic Questioning' *In Context,* http://www.context.org/ICLIB/IC40/Peavey.htm, last updated 29 June 2000, p. 1.
146 C. Elliott, *Comfortable Compassion* (London: Hodder &Stoughton, 1987), pp. 153–154.
147 M. Strom, *Reframing Paul* (Illinois: IVP, 2000), p. 189.
148 M. Strom, p. 183.
149 M. Strom, p. 183.
150 M. Strom, p 187.
151 C. Smidt, *Religion As Social Capital* (Waco: Baylor University Press, 2003), pp. 19–31.
152 P. Kaldor, K. Castle and R. Dixon, *Connections For Life: National Church Life Survey* (Adelaide: Open Book Publishers, 2002), pp. 54–60.
153 C. Smidt, *Religion As Social Capital* (Waco: Baylor University Press, 2003), pp. 94, 96.
154 P. Kaldor, K. Castle and R. Dixon, *Connections For Life: National Church Life Survey* (Adelaide: Open Book Publishers, 2002), p. 58.

155 R. Putnam, *Bowling Alone* (New York: Simon & Schuster, 2001), pp. 66, 68.
156 R. Putnam, pp. 74, 77–78.
157 P. Kaldor, K. Castle and R. Dixon, *Connections For Life: National Church Life Survey* (Adelaide: Open Book Publishers, 2002), p. 59.
158 P. Kaldor, *First Look In The Mirror: National Church Life Survey* (Homebush: ANZEA, 1992), p. 58.
159 P. Kaldor, p. 55.
160 R. Putnam, *Bowling Alone* (New York: Simon & Schuster, 2001), pp. 361–362.
161 G Lovell, *The Church And Community Development* (London: Grail, 1980), p. 53.
162 G. Lovell, p. 43.
163 This structure is comprised of a complex network of triangles that form a roughly spherical surface. The more complex the network of triangles, the more closely the dome approximates the shape of a true sphere. By using triangles of various sizes, a sphere can be symmetrically divided by thirty-one great circles. A great circle is the largest circle that can be drawn around a sphere, like the lines of longitude around the earth, or the equator. Each of these lines divide the sphere into two halves, hence the term 'geodesic', which is from the Latin meaning 'earth dividing'. From M. Amiano, viewed 10/11/07 <http://www.insite.com.br/rodrigo/bucky/buckminster_fuller.html>
164 http://mathworld.wolfram.com/Triangulation.html viewed 10/11/07.
165 http://www.gpsworlds.com/ viewed 10/11/07.
166 T. Atlee, *The Tao Of Democracy* (Cranston: The Writers' Collective, RI, 2003), p. 1.
167 T. Atlee, pp. 6–9.
168 A. Kelly and S. Sewell, *With Head, Heart And Hand* (Brisbane: Boolarong, 1989), pp. 62–64.
169 R. Putnam, *Bowling Alone* (New York: Simon & Schuster, 2001), pp. 92–94.
170 P. Palmer, *The Company Of Strangers* (New York: Crossroad, 1985), pp. 40–1.
171 P. Palmer, p. 41.
172 P. Palmer, pp. 41–2.

173 P. Palmer, p. 42.
174 P. Palmer, p. 43.
175 P. Palmer, p. 43.
176 P. Palmer, pp. 43–4.
177 P. Palmer, pp. 44–5.
178 P. Palmer, pp. 45-6.
179 P. Palmer, p. 45.
180 P. Palmer, p. 64.
181 P. Palmer, p. 67.
182 W. Carey. Originally spoken in his sermon to the Baptist Association meeting in Northampton, England, May 30, 1792, cited by W. Finnemore, (*The Story of a Hundred Years: 1823-1923* (Oxford: University Press, 1923), p. 14.
183 R. Putnam, *Bowling Alone* (New York: Touchstone Books, 2000), p. 201–2, 283.
184 R. Putnam, p. 212–3.
185 R. Putnam, p. 243.
186 R. Putnam, p. 222.
187 R. Putnam, p. 237.
188 R. Putnam, p. 242.
189 R. Putnam, p. 228.
190 G. Lovell, *The Church And Community Development* (London: Grail, 1980), p. 12.
191 G. Lovell, p. 51.
192 G. Lovell, p. 52.
193 For detailed scholarly evidence of this, see M. Strom, *Reframing Paul* (Downers Grove: IVP, 2000), pp. 159–181.
200 As he said in Matthew 11:28; John 16:23–4.
195 M. Schluter, 'Relationism — pursuing a biblical vision for society' www.jubilee-centre.org Vol. 6, No. 4, December 1997.
196 Report of the BCC Study Commission on Trinitarian Doctrine Today, *The Forgotten Trinity* (London: British Council of Churches, 1989), p. 16.
197 M. Schluter, 'Relationism — pursuing a biblical vision for society' www.jubilee-centre.org Vol. 6, No. 4, December 1997.
198 M. Schluter.

199 M. Schluter.
200 H. Nouwen, *Reaching Out* (New York: Doubleday, 1975), pp. 48–51.
201 J. Vanier, *Community And Growth* (Homebush: St Paul, 1989), pp. 31–32.
202 M. S. Peck, *The Different Drum* (London: Rider, 1987), pp. 61–62.
203 J. Vanier, *Community And Growth* (Homebush: St Paul, 1989), pp. 20–22.
204 J. Cobb and H. Daley, *For The Common Good* (Boston: Beacon Press, 1992), p. 172.
205 M. S. Peck, *The Different Drum* (London: Rider, 1987), p. 63.
206 A. Etzioni, *The Spirit Of Community* (New York: Simon and Schuster, 1993), pp. 144–147.
207 http://www.parliamentofreligions.org/index.cfm?n=4&sn=4 viewed 8.8.08.

www.ingramcontent.com/pod-product-compliance
Lightning Source LLC
Chambersburg PA
CBHW081231170426
43198CB00017B/2723